MW00397676

WHITNEY HOUSTON
One Moment in Time

WHITNEY HOUSTON
One Moment in Time

by
Richard Seal

BRITANNIA PRESS PUBLISHING

Copyright © Richard Seal. 1994
First published in Great Britain in 1994 by Britannia Press Publishing,
a division of Britannia Crest International Ltd.

All rights reserved. No part of this publication may be reproduced, stored in a retrieval
system or transmitted in any form or by any means electronic, mechanical, photocopying,
recording or otherwise, without the prior permission in writing from the publisher.

British Library Cataloguing in Publication Data. A catalogue record for this book is
available from the British Library.
        Seal
        Whitney Houston. *One Moment in Time*

        ISBN 0-9519937-8-X

Printed and bound in Great Britain by Biddles Ltd, Surrey.
Distribution: Bookpoint Ltd, Oxon.

Britannia Press Publishing, Britannia Crest International Ltd,
44 Chalk Farm Road, London NW1 8AN

*This book is dedicated
to Beryl Seal*

Thank you to the following, without whom
this book could not have been possible;

———————————————

James Constantinou - for helping with the research.

David Minns - for invaluable help and support.

André Delanchy - for being tolerant and patient.

Thanks also to:

George, Janet and Jan Seal - Antony Webb - Gina Walters -Mel Brown -
Andy, Jonathan and anyone else who I've unintentionally forgotten but who
either gave me support or encouragement in any way what so ever...

CONTENTS

Part four

Introduction

Whitney Houston's career achievements to date have been, by anyone's standards, quite remarkable. She has achieved peaks of success and attained respect within her chosen field far greater than almost any other female artist before her. Record sales figures have evolved to produce multi-million selling albums and she has become the recipient of countless prestigious and acclaimed awards.

Her beginnings remain a far cry from the sort of luxurious living and life style that she now enjoys, although she is one of the few not to forget where she came from and will still refer back to the early days and reflect on the momentous achievements she has attained. Her family's mightily impressive musical background and the previous achievements of family members such as mother Cissy Houston, aunt Dionne Warwick and close family friend Aretha Franklin, may suggest that all she had to do was merely enter a recording studio and a successful career would be tailor made for her, and yet, because of this, she has still had to prove herself to both her contemporaries and critics alike, perhaps even more so. Her early career achievements make for both fascinating and astonishing reading.

Her debut album entitled 'Whitney Houston' has become the biggest ever selling album by a female artist in the world, and to date has racked up the incredible total of over eighteen million copies sold worldwide.

She is often categorised as being in some sort of competition with Madonna, but in comparison, Madonna's first album comes nowhere near to match that sales figure, nor could it climb higher in the American album charts than Number 8, whereas Whitney's was a Number 1. Another Whitney achievement that is unparalleled and un-matched by any other solo artist, or indeed group, is the incredible run of having attained seven consecutive Number 1 singles in the American Billboard charts. A feat not even achieved by the legendary Beatles in their heyday, or by The Bee Gees, who during the 1970's were perhaps the biggest band in America.

Whitney has also entered and seemingly effortlessly succeeded in that notorious graveyard for Rock star legends, the film business. Her appearance in the multi million dollar grossing film 'The Body guard', saw her emerge triumphantly on the back of fair and often rave reviews. Indeed, a rare thing for someone primarily noted for their singing prowess, to achieve. She has also won many prestigious and coveted awards, including two Emmy's and looks to continue that trend in the coming years.

Recently married and the extremely proud mother of a happy and bouncing baby girl, Bobbi, Whitney's career continues, and a new chapter opens in the life of this exciting and invigorating young woman, Whitney Houston.

In the book 'One Moment in Time', we'll go back to learn about her early life, her incredibly supportive mother Cissy and those who have helped to make Whitney into the superstar that she is today.

Part one

The early years

Whitney Elizabeth Houston was born in Newark, New Jersey, on August 9th, 1963. Her mother's choice of her young daughter's slightly unusual Christian name was inspired by a character in her favourite U.S. soap opera of the time, and was favoured due to its spark of originality and the fact it was unique. She is the youngest of three children and has two elder brothers, Michael, who works with her and Gary, who is a professional basketball player in America.

Whitney Houston grew up around a whole wealth of talented and dedicated professionals in the world of music, perhaps none more so than her mother Cissy Houston. That, along with the other talented musical members of her family, later promoted Whitney to declare in an interview that *"Music was instilled in me when I was still in nappies. It's my heritage."*

In the early days, the young Whitney would often accompany her mother when she went on one of her many recording engagements, singing back-up vocals for such greats as Elvis Presley and Wilson Pickett. This was to give Whitney the familiarity within the studio environment that she would make her own later in life, in such domineering fashion.

In the early days of Whitney's childhood, her mother was practically living in the studio, working as a respected and admired session and backing singer. Cissy was also one of the founder members, and still active today as a contributory, of The New Hope Baptist Choir based in New Jersey, where the family lived.

Cissy, actually christened Emily 'Cissy' Drinkard Houston,

grew up in New Jersey's Newark and, shortly after her mother died when she was nine, she found herself living *"basically in the same house"* as her nieces Dee Dee and Dionne Warwick.

Cissy, along with her five brothers and sisters, was regularly to be found performing as a musical group known as the Drinkard's. It was such a close knit and tight community that if on any occasion any of them was ill, either Dee Dee or Dionne would step in and take one of the brothers' or sisters' place. It wasn't until her early teens, however, that Cissy began to actively pursue what would eventually become her Gospel stronghold. Both her's and her family's religious transformation is widely credited as being one of the primary reasons that so much talent in depth and diversity has emerged over the years, from her and her immediate family.

Whitney's mother knew an awful lot about the intricacies of the music business from a very early age, having turned professional at the remarkably young age of six when she joined as a fully fledged member of the family Gospel singing group the Drinkard Sisters. This experience not only gave Whitney, when the time arrived, a huge knowledge of what lay before her but it was also a large factor and influence on her undeniable eagerness to sing and to entertain. *"I think I got my emotions from Gospel singing, from my mother instilling it in me at an early age"*, Whitney would later say about the early days and occasions such as her first solo singing experience, where as an eight year old she sang, *'Guide Me, O Thou Great Jehovah'*, in her mother's New Hope Baptist Choir church.

Apart from singing with such greats as Presley and Pickett, Cissy Houston also made a huge name for herself through her work with many of the greatest soul singers of the sixties such as Dionne Warwick (Whitney's aunt), and Aretha Franklin (a close family friend, and Whitney's God-mother), and to whom Cissy contributed the distinctive and powerful backing vocals for one of her biggest hit singles *'Respect'*.

The young Whitney would often be accompanying her mother during these recording sessions and it is more often than not that she will turn to the Aretha Franklin one when asked what the most enjoyable aspects of her childhood were. She is quoted as remembering the Aretha Franklin sessions as being by far the most energetic and full of emotions. She also remembers how quickly they were completed, more often than not in just one or two takes.

She later recalled how Aretha would *"just sing it live. At those times you had the band in the room with you and the backing singers. And you did it all in a day"*. She would also gain a lot of what would ultimately prove to be invaluable experience, because of the time she was spending around the studios with her mother. This would eventually be put into practice when she herself began to contribute actively to others and indeed go on to make her own recordings.

The late 1960's were spent by Cissy Houston in an exhaustive but enjoyable period in which she toured consistently as back up singer for Dionne Warwick and contributed to the recordings of such future classic singles as *'Do You Know The Way To San José'* and *'I Say A Little Prayer'*. In the early days, Whitney was greatly influenced and encouraged by Dionne, and she would sit glued to the television set whenever her aunt appeared to sing one of her many million selling hit singles. By 1968, after many years of singing on other peoples' records to enormous ovation but little public knowledge of who she was, Cissy formed her own Pop-Gospel Quartet under the name of 'The Sweet Inspirations'. Despite being a huge and popular live act they were not however to find the success they deserved through the mainstream outlets of radio and television, due in part to the overtly 'religious' nature of their recordings. The R&B styled recording they made, with songs such as *'Brand New Lover'*, *'Why Am I Treated So Bad'* and *'What The World Needs Now Is Love'*, have since become collectors' items today, when the attitude of the media to such offerings is of course far more accepted and forward looking in their approach.

Cissy continued into the early 1970's still as a much respected and admired backing vocalist and collaborator. Although she was in many ways unfortunate not to become a huge success in her own right, she did however continue to help make many other artists' records just that little more distinctive and distinguishable from the rest.

In the early 70's, she helped out on Linda Ronstadt's acclaimed *'Heart Like A Wheel'*, and went on to make Bette Midler's *'Do You Wanna Dance'*, another critically if not especially commercially successful record. But, despite these triumphs, she was not destined to make it in the successful manner that had been expected of her as a solo artist.

However, she is to this day still sought after by many of today's more popular black soul artists when they are making records and is often to be found with a credit on such greats as Luther Vandross, contributing vocals when he makes a new album.

Whitney's parents divorced when she was in her early teens, not an easy time for any child and although Whitney was obviously disturbed by what happened, she never really let it come between the strong relationships she had with both her mother and her father. Her father, John Houston, eventually became, and remains to this day, her business manager. She recalls how after her parents' divorce that if she appeared to be paying a lot of attention and giving a lot of love to one of them in particular, the other would become slightly jealous. But they ultimately both knew how much their daughter loved them and so this was usually easily resolved.

Whitney herself says that her mother was often strict and domineering, an extremely caring mother but with the capacity at the same time to often be a slightly over-bearing one. Whitney relates a story of how this was often put into operation when talking about it in later years, when she remembers how *"chewing gum or sitting with your legs open were considered unacceptable, and I'd better not come in from the back-yard with my knees scratched."* She goes on to tell how she was never allowed to date boys while she was younger or wear make-up. This was to transcend itself into her school life as well, where she admits she was not given a particularly easy time by the other kids and was often picked upon due to her mother's obsession with sending her to school immaculately turned out in pretty pinafore dresses and bows in her hair.

Her classmates, particularly the other girls, would often pick on her because they thought her hair was too long and her skin too light. The young Whitney would often get around these problems in novel if not uncommon ways. For example, she would often take a pair of jeans to school, hidden out of sight from her mother in her school bag, until a safe distance had occurred, in which time she would quickly whip them out and change into them so she would not stand out so much from the other kids who would also assume this teenage fashion of jeans and T-shirts. This ploy by Whitney was to prove not only effective in making her feel more a part of the school she was attending, it also stopped the bullying and teasing that she had previously had to endure. It gave her a much needed degree of conformity among her classmates. She herself was later to recall that *"Blue jeans saved my ass a lot of the time."*

The need to conform and be a part of the more wide-spread world around her, led Whitney into something of a rebellious period when she was in her early teens. She admits herself, *"from fourteen to eighteen I was almost out of control, doing what I wanted. I had an independent streak because I was working, singing with my mother and doing some modelling. I wanted to find out about the world. My mother couldn't control me any more."*

This came to something of a head when she was 16, she says, *"my mother used to say to me, you're not going to make it to 17, I can feel it."* When Whitney asked why, her mother replied that it was because if she went on the way she was, she was going to kill her! She does however admit that this never totally manifested itself in any long term or destructive way, towards her relationship with her family, and says that despite what happened, her mother was still always there for her and provided Whitney more often than not with the shoulder she needed to cry on or the ears in which she needed someone to listen to her. Like many children of that age, she was merely going through difficult times, but in retrospect, she explains about her relationship with her mother, *"If something is bothering me, she automatically knows it. She doesn't guess, she knows. It's magical and it lets me know how powerful the mother-child link is."*

Whitney was not what would be described as being an exceptionally talented or gifted student (her vocation was to be in other areas). Surprisingly, she did not even excel in music lessons, although this can be explained in part by the fact that she was regularly spending up to four days a week singing in the church and so she wasn't particularly keen when lessons at school were revolving around the same subject.

However, her school life was not as dissimilar to many of the other students in that she is still able to recall that special moment when she had her first kiss. When asked about it some years later she recalled, *"I was 12 or 13 and it was with a boy called Craig, who I still see. A great kiss from a great kisser. He knew he was the first! A memorable moment."*

As bestowed upon many youngsters, young Whitney was

often given nicknames, these included 'Nippy', by her father, who called her that because she was always running around, and also 'Lizzy' or 'Whit' from friends at school.

Surprisingly, her first aspirations toward the future were not to be a singer, instead she wanted to become a teacher or a vet when she was a young child, although this soon was replaced by singing when she realised just how much she enjoyed it.

Her singing career really began to materialise in a spectacular fashion when at the age of eight she sang her first real solo in public. This was in her mother's New Baptist church choir although she also regularly sang in public as part of her mother's cabaret act. Her performance though, when she sang *'Guide Me, O Thou Great Jehovah'* still sticks in her mind as being a special and treasured memory. She recalled after the event how she was both thrilled but at the same time slightly disturbed by the reaction she created within the congregation, half of whom were in tears after her stirring performance.

Another big public performance came at the age of 14 when her mother Cissy was performing at New York's Town Hall and the young Whitney came on stage to sing part of the song *'Tomorrow'* from the musical *'Annie'* to a rapturous response. Whitney remembers of her performance of *'Tomorrow'* that during it *"people rushed the stage, I kind of backed up. I was scared of the intensity."*

During this time, Whitney met Robin Crawford who was to become one of her closest friends and remains so to this day as her personal assistant. Robin was able to talk and discuss any problems with Whitney that she may be having, which to Whitney was a great comfort. Robin says of the early days, with a large degree of modesty that she was merely there for Whitney, and that she did a lot of listening which is what Whitney needed.

Around this time, Whitney would sing backing vocals as well as perform the odd duet with her mother. Her big moment when she was performing with her mother as part of a cabaret act was when she got the chance to sing a solo. This would usually be the song *'The Greatest Love Of All'*, from the 1977 movie *'The Greatest'*. The film, a bioptic about and starring Muhammed Ali was something of a flop at the box office, but the song most definitely stood out. The song was originally recorded by George Benson, to a fair degree of critical appraisal and success, but it was not really until Whitney herself re-recorded it for her debut album, that it became a major triumph and a Number 1 single throughout the world. Because of this attention and admiration, her parents were keen that she should finish her education before thinking about pursuing any sort of long term or serious musical career. Despite her parents reservations however, by the age of 15, she was something of a regular around the studio environment, singing backing vocals for soul greats of the day like Chaka Khan and Lou Rawls.

First steps

Whitney's parents' insistence that she should finish her education before looking toward her much anticipated musical career was fine, except that it didn't quite work out that way. Whilst walking down Seventh Avenue in New York, Whitney (who was then aged 16) and her mother, were approached by a man who asked Whitney if she modelled. She said *"no"*, but he told her that she should seriously consider it because she was tall and very beautiful. He went on to recommend the name of the Click agency who were looking for models at the time. Whitney visited them and was offered a contract on the spot.

She modelled for a while, becoming a cover girl at the age of 17, appearing in and on the covers of magazines such as 'Cosmopolitan', 'Glamour' and 'Seventeen' and earning a lucrative contract with the cosmetic manufacturer Revlon.

Although it was not in her career plan, modelling did provide Whitney with among other things a very attractive salary. She was able to earn around five thousand dollars a day for just two hours work. However, her heart was not in modelling and after a short period of time she soon realised that it was not for her. She later said, *"I found it degrading, it wasn't a life that I wanted to live."* She also told how her mother had been against her modelling and how Whitney had realised she was right when she said that the women who did that and relied on their looks to such extent were the ultimate losers, when you see how many of them turn out, and how real beauty lives in something such as a smile.

Whilst pursuing her career as a glamour model, Whitney was also taking her first tentative steps towards what would later become a large part of both her repertoire and her career, acting. She was regularly taking lessons in New York to help her general performance and found that this was very beneficial in helping to create a presence on stage and translate the lyrics of a song into more of a performance for the audience.

These lessons were of great benefit to her in other ways as well. She was soon offered the chance to put them into practice when she was given minor roles on a couple of American shows at the time, *'Silver Spoons'* and *'Gimmie A Break'*.

Although they were only small and relatively insignificant parts for Whitney with regards to her later achievements, it was still an important step up the ladder for her and would be of enormous benefit to her career in the long run. Taking it slowly and not accepting everything that was offered to her just for the sake of it. This tactical approach to her development had been the work and suggestion of her management team, Gene Harvey and Seymour Flics, with whom she signed a management contract at age seventeen, two years after her first major foray into the music business and her first notable recording. They had seen the enormous potential in Whitney from a very early age but were determined not to force her into any half thought out or rash decisions where her career was concerned. They were far more interested in helping to carefully develop and nurture this talent.

After the acting lessons, the small parts in television shows and the great buzz that was already doing the rounds regarding this new singing sensation, the management team of Harvey and Flics had to deal with many attempts from record companies and other organisations to try and gain Whitney's talents for themselves. This would have to put itself on hold for a while though as the main thing that was decided and as Harvey would himself later explain during an interview with The Los Angeles Times, *"The most important thing was for Whitney to continue to develop as an artist in an unhurried and un-pressured way."*

First major recordings

The huge amount of experience and advice both her mother and others around her, with regards to working in a studio environment had proved invaluable to Whitney. Perhaps none more so than when she went into the studio for the first time. Whitney Houston's recording debut was actually made as far back as 1979 when she sang lead vocals for The Michael Zager Band's *'Life's A Party'*, the title track of their second album which emerged on the Private Stock record label. This momentous occasion occurred when Whitney was fifteen years of age and began to cause quite a stir at the time with many other artists, management people and record companies, all becoming aware of her potential. In fact Michael Zager himself was so impressed with Whitney's performance on the *'Life's A Party'* track that he was eager to sign Whitney onto a recording contract. The idea was discussed but ultimately rejected by Whitney, primarily on the advice of her mother Cissy, who was only too aware of the perils involved in getting into the music business at too early an age.

During the next few years, she was also to make occasional 'guest' appearances on other peoples' records including singing on the track *'Eternal Love'* for the *'Paul Jabara and Friends'* album and also singing on the track *'Memories'* for the group Material on their *'One Down'* album.

Another one of Whitney's first recordings was with American Soul star Teddy Pendergrass with whom she dueted on the 1984 album track and eventual single, *'Hold Me'*.

This was to really push the young singer to the fore-front and help to mould her career in the early days. She collaborated with Teddy Pendergrass for the smooth and silky 1984 duet *'Hold Me'*, which became a wide spread success, both critically and commercially. Although the single only reached Number 44 in Britain, it was very well received by the critics and helped to gain recognition at this early stage in her career for Whitney in this country.

From a young age, partly because of her obvious potential and the pulling power she already had, many parties where interested in trying to secure Whitney's signature on record deals, etc... Whitney recalls, *"people were interested in me from the time I was 15. I remember many long drawn out meetings."* As a result of one of these meetings however, she finally signed to Clive Davis of Arista Records.

Clive Davis had previously signed and helped to mould into huge stars such famous names as Janis Joplin and two of the people most instrumental in Whitney's career, Aretha Franklin and Dionne Warwick.

The signing of Whitney Houston to Arista Records took place in 1983 when Gerry Griffith, then director of R & B music within the A & R department of Arista Records, arranged for Whitney to audition for the label's president, Clive Davis. It transpired that Whitney would be singing with her mother Cissy at Seventh Avenue South in New York, and that would become the location for the historic first meeting between the two. Whitney was scheduled to play a 30 minute set... One of the songs which she would sing would be one of her future American Number 1, *'The Greatest Love Of All'*.

Griffith, who had previously seen her perform elsewhere and who arranged for Clive Davis to go and see her had said of Whitney, *"She was the most phenomenal original talent I had seen in years, I set up a showcase for Clive. I said to him, 'I'm not even going to ask you. I'm setting up a showcase for this young lady. You will be absolutely blown away!"* Which Clive Davis certainly was, arranging a contract for this blossoming talent the following day.

One of Clive Davis first major decisions regarding Whitney's future career was that she would not be thrust out into the spotlight straight away but that she should be gradually helped and nurtured into that position. One of Whitney's managerial team, Gene Harvey, later explained, *"It was a matter of searching for the right material and the right producers. It was Clive's philosophy and ours as well that we should not push this girl out there straight away. We decided to wait and to do the best job we could, and so subsequently that meant that if it took a little longer than usual, then so be it."*

Clive Davis is more often than not described as being a 'songmaster', with a particular penchant for ballads. But more importantly than that he was the man who saw in Whitney a huge talent just waiting to be fully developed and explored. Clive Davis was reportedly impressed by her 'looks and lungs', on their first encounter. He is often credited for having 'created' Whitney but this is something he vehemently denies, stating quite truly that if the talent was not there in the first place then there would have been nothing to nurture.

Talking on the subject when asked about it, Davis has said in the past, *"I didn't create Whitney, although I did work with her on a creative level. I was involved in picking the right material with her, choosing the right producers, waiting until the top people were free to work with her. I saw a rare combination of talent and beauty."*

Of course, Clive Davis has been very important and instrumental in helping Whitney Houston get where she is today, something which is a talent within itself, and so perhaps he should be congratulated for achieving that. Rumours of course abound concerning the working relationship between Whitney and Clive Davis, something that inevitably occurs when a star as big as she is, is involved. Some reports have allegedly suggested that Clive Davis actually owns the exclusive rights toward marketing Whitney, and that if he was to relinquish his position at the Arista Records label and leave, then he would be contractually entitled to take Whitney as well.

These talents that he earmarked for an impressive and long term career were important and over riding factors in his decision to surround Whitney with top producers, song writers and musicians when the time was ready to begin work on her debut album.

Before the release of her debut album, Whitney was to make her debut 'live' performance which took place in February, 1985. The 'Sweetwaters' club in New York was chosen as the perfect venue for this momentous occasion and America's most influential and fashionable papers and magazines were invited along to witness the occasion. One of the members of the audience that night, along with Clive Davis, was respected songwriter Michael Masser, composer of *'The Greatest Love Of All'*, one of the undoubted highlights of Whitney's 'live' performances at the time.

Michael Masser later recalled how he was walking into the Sweetwater's club when he became aware that was what Whitney was singing on stage at that moment, and he later was to recall how, *"she was singing my song 'Greatest Love Of All' as we walked in and the performance just blew my mind."*

The show was a huge success by any standards and led the critic of the influential New York Post to comment that, *"what is happiest to those who have watched her grow is that she's not just a voice; with gestures and with poise, she takes command of her stage and her moment, and thus her time is limitless. When at the end of a song she opens her arms, roses cannot fill them - the universe rushes in to embrace her"*. Fine praise indeed, and sentiments that were similarly echoed by People magazine in that same year who were moved to state that *"it will take an act of congress to keep this woman from becoming a megastar."*

Debut album
'Whitney Houston'

When Whitney Houston's debut album, entitled *'Whitney Houston'* arrived in the record stores in late 1985, the anticipation preceding its release was immense. Much was expected of it in the way that it performed chart and sales-wise. But few could have really expected or anticipated just how successful it would actually prove to be.

It would eventually go on to sell over eighteen million copies worldwide (and continues to sell at a steady rate today) and yield a whole clutch of million selling and Number 1 singles, for both Whitney and her record company.

The album's release worldwide had been heralded by the first of these million selling singles, *'Saving All My Love For You'*. In Britain and indeed throughout the rest of the world, the single was an instant success, reaching Number 1 in practically every country in which it was granted a release. The single hit Number 1 in Britain in late November, 1985 and stayed there into December for two weeks, spending an impressive sixteen weeks on the chart in the process.

'Saving All My Love For You' was written by Michael Masser and Gerry Goffin some years previously and was produced by Masser himself for inclusion on Whitney's debut album. The song was originally recorded by the husband and wife singing team of Marilyn McCoo and Billy Davis Jr, for their first album on a new deal they had signed in America with CBS Records.

They themselves had in the past achieved notable American success, particularly in 1977 when they gained a Number 1 single with *'You Don't Have To Be A Star (To Be In My Show)'* which apart from being an American Number 1 single also went on to win the duo a Grammy award for best R & B Vocal Performance in the category for best Duo, Group or Chorus performance.

Michael Masser who actually produced both versions of the song *'Saving All My Love For You'* made a few subtle changes to its structure when the recording process for Whitney's version was taking place. He later explained, *"I altered the song somewhat, took out the second bridge, changed a few things, and then when it was finished told Gene Harvey, (of Whitney's management company): That's the single, that's going to be your first Number 1."*

The single was accompanied by a suitably tasteful and seductive video reflecting the stylish and sophisticated mode of the song's music and lyrics. It was, indeed, as producer Michael Masser had predicted, also soon to hit Number 1 in America, becoming the first in what would become a long and unprecedented run of consecutive Number 1 singles there for Whitney.

As for the album's music, the pattern began to emerge very early on with the first track *'You Give Good Love'*. Whitney's vocals soared over a slinky and smooth musical arrangement that would continue throughout the album's duration, and go some way to defining what would unmistakably become 'her sound'. *'You Give Good Love'* was actually Whitney's first single to be pulled from the album, a fact which is often overlooked due to the phenomenal performances and success achieved by its subsequent singles.

Written by LaLa and produced by Kashif, *'You Give Good Love'*'s release, particularly in America, was designed to give Whitney a noticeable position and standing within the black music charts over there.

Clive Davis later explained the thinking behind releasing *'You Give Good Love'* as the debut single from the album, saying, *"we wanted to establish her in the black marketplace first, otherwise you can fall between cracks, where top 40 radio won't play you and R & B radio won't consider you their own. We felt that 'You Give Good Love' would be, at the very least, a major black hit, though we didn't think it would cross over the way it did."*

'You Give Good Love' did indeed 'cross over' well to all charts it

was consider eligible for, particularly the pop charts, where it was eventually to reach Number 3 on the Billboard Hot 100 in July of 1985.

Whitney's vocals on the album's second track, *'Thinking About You'* were even more defined, dominating the sound with an authoritative air, over what actually turned out to be a slightly more subdued musical arrangement.

The album featured two duets with ex-Jackson Five star, Jermaine, who also produced for Whitney the two tracks on which they collaborated, the up-tempo *'Take Good Care Of My Heart'*, and the smoother ballad *'Nobody Loves Me Like You Do'*.

Whilst both of these duets with Jermaine Jackson were pleasant and likeable, they didn't quite match, however, the album's other dual project, Whitney's duet with Teddy Pendergrass on the albums closing track *'Hold Me'*. Whitney had of course sung with Teddy previously on his album and here was returning the favour for him on her own album.

One of the album's many undoubted highlights was the up-tempo strains of the Narada Michael Walden produced track, *'How Will I Know'*. The pop orientated feel of the song was probably somewhat instrumental in the decision to release this song as the album's third single. It was accompanied by a suitably 'up' video and in America, the large amount of exposure afforded to the video by MTV, helped it to follow in the footsteps of *'Saving All My Love For You'* to the top of the American Billboard Top 100 singles chart.

The song also performed well in the British charts when released in January of 1986, climbing as high as Number 5 and spending twelve weeks on the chart.

Ironically, *'How Will I Know'* had not originally been intended for use by Whitney as it had in fact been written by writers George Merrill, Shannon Rubican and Narada Michael Walden with another artist, no less than Janet Jackson, in mind. Janet Jackson's management advisors however passed on the song deciding that it was not the sort of material for which they were looking for Janet to record. This disappointed one of the writers, George Merrill, who later said that, *"we were pretty upset, (by the rejection), because we thought it was perfect for Janet Jackson at the time. We had written it with her completely in mind."*

'*How Will I Know*' was, though, too strong a song to be left idily sitting on the shelf and a cassette of it finally fell into the hands of Gerry Griffith at Arista Records. He instantly thought it would be a perfect song for inclusion on Whitney's album.

He would later say of the decision to record it for Whitney's debut album, "*We had a lot of R & B based tunes, we had a few ballads, but we didn't really have a pop crossover song. But when I heard 'How Will I Know' I said, this is absolutely perfect. I played it to Clive Davis and he fell in love with it as well.*"

Once the decision had been taken to record the song for the album, the idea was suggested also that it would be a good idea for one of the song's writers, who was also a much sought after and respected producer, Narada Michael Walden, to come in and produce it.

Narada Michael Walden was and indeed still is very much in demand as a producer, however, and at the time he was busy working together with Aretha Franklin on her album, '*Who's Zoomin' Who?*' When the proposal came forward for him to produce the track he was initially somewhat reluctant to tackle the task, later explaining that, "*Gerry Griffith called and begged me to produce this song ('How Will I Know'), for Whitney Houston. I had no idea who Whitney Houston was at the time, in fact none of us did. I had to explain to him that the Aretha record was a very important album and it wasn't the kind of thing we wanted to take time out of. He persuaded me to listen to the song though and to give it some serious thought.*"

Another fairly lacklustre reception to the idea of Whitney recording '*How Will I Know*' also came from one of the other song's writers, George Merrill, who said, "*I wasn't very familiar with her family background, I didn't realise that even at that time there was a pretty big industry buzz going on about her future.*"

After listening to the track Narada Michael Walden decided that it might be possible to do something with it, perhaps with Whitney. However, one of his criteria for taking the job on board was that he wanted to make some changes to the structure of the song. In order to do this he had to seek permission from the two other co-writers, Merrill and Shannon Rubican. They, however, were not keen on having their work tampered with and initially refused permission for the song to be changed in any way.

This all made Narada Michael Walden become disillusioned

with the whole project and he began to lose what initial little interest he had in it. Walden said, *"I called Gerry Griffith and said this whole thing is not going to happen. First of all, the songwriters don't want me to touch their song and second of all, I don't know who Whitney Houston is. I don't have time to mess with her."*

Walden, however, persevered with the song and eventually found a way to persuade Merrill and Rubican to approve it and indeed write some more lyrics to an added verse after Walden had composed it.

Eventually, the new shape of the song started to emerge although in somewhat different form to the original. Merrill later said of this new version of their original song, *"It was a pretty different version from our demo. At first listening we really didn't get it."*

Shannon Rubican herself was also unsure at first, but later admitted that although it took a bit of getting used to, in the end the song worked very well. She herself would later say of the finished product that, *"It turned out fine in the end. The reason we balked at first though about it was that we hadn't ever co-written with anybody like that before. We didn't know Narada and had never met him. We certainly weren't used to the idea of someone changing one of our songs. But we were happy enough in the end with the final outcome."*

Whitney's vocals for the song were recorded in one day at studios in New York. The following day her mother Cissy also came into the studio to sing backing vocals on it, with the intention of Whitney singing them as well. This though took a bit of persuading on Whitney's part as she was happy enough just to sit and watch her mother's enormous talents at work in the studio environment. It took some persuading on Narada Michael Walden's part to get Whitney into the studio as well to join in on the background vocals, but as he later explained the end product made it well worth it.

Of the recording session with both Whitney and her mother together he said, *"I asked Whitney to sing on the background session, she was reluctant though because she wanted to enjoy hearing her mother sing, I said, 'No, get out there too and sing,' so she did. The background sounds incredible."* Clive Davis was equally impressed by the final product, proclaiming the finished record as being, *"A ten"*.

Another one of the album's more durable and long term popular songs was the engulfing, power charged qualities of the classic sounding *'All At Once'*. The song was co-written by celebrated US soul star Jeffrey Osborne, who in the early 1980's enjoyed a run of chart success on his own merits with singles such as *'Stay With Me Tonight'* and *'On The Wings Of Love'*.

Along with *'Saving All My Love For You'*, another of the album's more durable songs that is still widely played on radio stations around the world today, has proved to be the song which gave Whitney another British hit, (reaching the Top 10 in May of 1986), and yet another in the string of those American Number 1's, *'The Greatest Love Of All'*.

'The Greatest Love Of All', again part -written by writer Michael Masser, but this time in collaboration with Linda Creed, hit Number 1 in America in May of 1988 and remained there solidly for three weeks, seeing off challenges for the Number 1 spot at the time by songs such as The Pet Shop Boy's *'West End Girls'* and Janet Jackson's *'What Have You Done For Me Lately'* in the process.

Apart from the song itself contributing to Whitney's record breaking run of American Number 1's, it also helped to give her another record breaking achievement prior to this, when by getting to Number 1 Whitney became the first ever female solo artist in American chart history to achieve three Number1 hit singles from a debut album. An extraordinary accomplishment for a singer so young at the time and with so relatively little experience of the business.

The enormous success of the single *'Greatest Love Of All'* very nearly never happened at all though as there were no plans for the song to be taken from the album for single release, but public pressure in the end saw the record company realise that there was a huge demand for the song.

Indeed, originally the song could be found as the B side to Whitney's debut American release *'You Give Good Love'* and its release as a single only came about after enormous public pressure forced its re-release as an independent single. This was due to the large demand to hear the song being requested by the public and played by radio stations. And of course, in the end, the re-release of the song proved to be a very wise decision.

The tactic employed for the album with the combination of different producers and writers had made for what was essentially an extremely consistent and strong collection of songs that gelled together well, making a seemingly effortless fine debut album.

All in all the album's huge achievements in both its record sales and its award winning feats, proved most conclusively what so many critics and public alike had predicted and expected, that Whitney Houston was a huge star in the making, and was most definitely here for a long stay.

The 'Whitney' album

Whitney's second album, titled somewhat confusingly after the first, 'Whitney', started what was to become its near two year residency in the British albums chart in June, 1987.

The album had been enormously anticipated by her now millions of devoted fans worldwide, whose un-abated eagerness for anything new that Whitney released, helped to propel the 'Whitney' album straight to the summit of the charts on its first week of release, a position it was to hold onto fielding off all comer's for a total of six weeks throughout the summer of 1987. This was to give Whitney her first British Number 1 album, although certainly not her last.

Again, in America, the release of the album was an occasion that was particularly momentous for Whitney.

Apart from selling millions of copies she was to become the first female artist in the history of the Billboard album charts there to have an album go straight into the charts at Number 1, surpassing the achievements of previously best selling female artists such as Madonna and Diana Ross, neither of whom, despite their record breaking and distinguished careers, were able to accomplish this particular feat.

Also, in becoming the first female artist in American recording history to have her album enter the charts at Number 1, she also joined an elite of a small number of other artists who had previously achieved this.

In case you're now wondering and to set the record straight, the other albums and the artists who have succeeded with this prior to Whitney are, firstly, Elton John, who has actually achieved it twice and even more impressively both times it was in the same year of 1975 with his two albums, 'Captain Fantastic and the Brown

Dirt Cowboy' and *'Rock Of The Westies'*; also, one of Whitney's great friends, Stevie Wonder who went straight to Number 1 in 1976 with his album, *'Songs In The Key Of Life'*, and Bruce Springsteen who was the last artist to do this prior to Whitney and who achieved the same feat some eleven years later than Stevie Wonder had done when in 1986 his *'Bruce Springsteen and The E Street Band Live - 1975-1985''* album crashed straight into the Billboard album charts at Number 1. Whitney was to become the fifth of this elite group which has now grown considerably in numbers, but that is mainly due to the changes that have been made with regards to how the American album chart is now compiled.

The release of the *'Whitney'* album had been preceded by her second British Number 1 single in May of 1987, *'I Wanna Dance With Somebody (Who Loves Me)'*.

The song, written by George Merrill and Shannon Rubican, who had previously helped to write an earlier Whitney chart topper, *'How Will I Know'* and who themselves went on to achieve an admirable degree of success with their debut album and its first single release, *'Waiting For A Star To Fall'*, a Top Ten hit in Britain under their adopted guise as Boy Meets Girl, was a two week chart topper for Whitney, during its eventual sixteen week run in the British charts.

Merrill and Rubican themselves were also beginning to become something of a hot item when they were connected in some way with a single's release.

Apart from now writing two of Whitney's chart toppers and scoring a degree of success in their own right, they themselves had previously sung on an American Number 1 single when they contributed backing vocals on Denice Williams' chart topper *'Let's Hear It For The Boy'*, taken from the soundtrack to the film *Footloose* and an American Number 1 for two weeks in May, 1984.

It was actually as a result of the success of *'How Will I Know'* that the songwriting duo were asked to come up with another song for Whitney's new album.

Originally the song that gave George Merrill and Shannon Rubican their British top ten success as Boy Meets Girl, *'Waiting For A Star To Fall'* was intended by the duo to be a song for Whitney and the inspiration they got to write it was actually from an incident that occurred when they attended a Whitney concert at the eight thousand capacity open air Greek Theatre in Los Angeles.

Shannon Rubican later explained how the inspiration for the song came about when she said, *"We were at Whitney's concert at The Greek Theatre and she had just finished singing 'How Will I Know' and we just happened to look up at the sky while people were clapping and cheering and a star was falling".* *"We both saw it and so I pulled out my note pad and wrote the words 'Waiting For A Star To Fall' and then later we wrote the song around those words. We sent it off to Arista but they passed on it deciding it wasn't suitable as material for Whitney."*

Un-deterred by this minor set back the pair continued working on finding a song that would be ideal as potential block busting Whitney material and they were to succeed in finding it when they got the inspiration needed to come with *'I Wanna Dance With Somebody'.*

Later on, explaining the idea behind the song, Shannon Rubican said, *"I pictured somebody single wishing that they could find that special person for themselves. It wasn't, 'I wanna go down the disco and dance', really. It was, 'I wanna do that dance of life with somebody'. That was the thought behind the song. So we sent our demo version off to Clive Davis and he loved it."*

The same initial enthusiasm for the song didn't however come from the eventual producer, who again was Narada Michael Walden. He took a little more persuading with regards to the song's potential and at first wasn't too keen on having Whitney record it. He said of it, *"At first I thought it was too Country and Western sounding. It reminded me of a rodeo song with Olivia Newton-John singing".* *" I love Olivia Newton-John, but for Whitney Houston it didn't seem right. I felt the song needed a much more funkier feel. I slept, dreaming about it, woke up in the morning thinking about it, wondering what am I gonna do with this dance song. So, we just jumped in the water and lo and behold a magic record was born, Whitney just knocked it out and then I knew we had a good record."*

'I Wanna Dance With Somebody (Who Loves Me)' was also the fourth consecutive single by Whitney Houston to glide effortlessly to the top of the American Billboard Hot 100 when released there in June, 1987.

The feverish acceptance of the public to the release of *'I Wanna Dance With Somebody'*, greatly aided the album's release and largely helped to accelerate the already 'heavily in demand status' of the lady herself.

Many reviews of Whitney's second album were critical to the point of complaining that the collection of songs, when compared with those of the first album, meant that it was merely a case of the album forming part two of what already had come before. Most of the reviewers overlooking the patently obvious fact that there was, in fact, a huge worldwide market out there, eager and wanting the sort of music that Whitney was delivering so well to them.

But, although the album did deliver as its predecessor had done so competently before it, a large quota of up-tempo dance numbers coupled with her trade mark smooth and sultry balladeering, the songs were rather more thought out and on the whole far more mature and sophisticated this time.

This was in the main partly aided by Whitney herself, whose vocal performances were really beginning to show a new burst of exuberance and confidence in their execution of the chosen material.

This growth of confidence had been helped enormously by her having played her first large scale concerts all around the world, where she was to regularly sell out arenas holding ten thousand plus fans.

As for the album's music, after the infectious qualities that ran all over the '*I Wanna Dance With Somebody*' single, a big hit in the clubs throughout the country this time as well as on the radio, came the album's second new song, '*Just The Lonely Talking*'.

'*Just The Lonely Talking*' was another in Whitney's ever increasing line of silky ballads that she was starting to make her own, having that undeniable stamp of class, a subtle and un-clustered musical arrangement perfectly complementing Whitney's sure and authoritative vocal.

The second one of five tracks from the album to be granted release as a single in Britain was the show stopping power ballad, '*Didn't We Almost Have It All*'.

The biggest surprise, however, surrounding the release of '*Didn't We Almost Have It All*' as a single, was its relatively poor performance in sales and chart position, compared with many of Whitney's earlier singles.

It was in fact Whitney's first failure in five attempts as a solo artist to crack the British Top Ten of the singles chart, eventually stalling at a slightly disappointing Number 14 in August of 1987.

In America though, the release of *'Didn't We Almost Have It All'* as a single was an altogether different affair. It was soon destined to become Whitney's fifth consecutive Number 1 single there and also a fifth American Number 1 for writer Michael Masser.

'Didn't We Almost Have It All', Masser's fifth American Number 1 single as a writer, was a collaboration between him and another writer, Will Jennings, who himself was no stranger to reaching the heights of having written an American Number 1, having previously been involved in the writing of three other chart toppers; namely, Barry Manilow's 1977 Number 1 *'Looks Like We Made It'*, Joe Cocker and Jennifer Warnes three week Number 1 from the film *'An Officer and A Gentleman'*, *'Up Where We Belong'* in 1982 and a co-written effort with singer Steve Winwood in 1986 on the single *'Higher Love'* which was Number 1 for a solitary week in August of that year.

The writing of the song *'Didn't We Almost Have It All'* was not, however, an easy task for the pair.

Jennings later recalled how, *"Michael Masser and I worked on and off for years on that song. I don't know how many times I must have re-wrote bits of the tune, but, of course, it was well worth it in the end."*

The same fate was to occur in Britain as had done previously when *'Didn't We Almost Have It All'* was released, when another of the album's slower paced singles, *'Where Do Broken Hearts Go'* was released as a single the following year.

Like *'Didn't We Almost Have It All'* before it, it was also to peak in the British singles chart at a lower than average position for Whitney, again reaching Number 14, and spending an equally paltry, by Whitney's standards, eight weeks on the chart, when released in March, 1988.

Interestingly and very much bearing in mind that by now Whitney was regularly being hailed as 'Queen of the Ballad', *'Where Do Broken Hearts Go'* and *'Didn't We Almost Have It All'*'s relatively poor showings on the singles chart was making something of a mockery of that slightly stereo-typical sounding tag. The two songs had proved to be Whitney's weakest singles chart performances so far whilst both being very much from the school of big ballads that she was so famous for.

The other three tracks released from the album as singles, the aforementioned '*I Wanna Dance With Somebody (Who Loves Me)*', as well as the calypso sounding '*Love Will Save The Day*' and the slightly harder pushing 'live' favourite, '*So Emotional*' all had made, or were to make more of an impression on the singles charts in Britain, particularly position-wise as they all quite comfortably made the Top 10.

'*I Wanna Dance With Somebody*' had of course soared right to the top and previously hit Number One whilst the other two also performed very well, '*So Emotional*' becoming a Top 5 single in November of 1987, whilst '*Love Will Save The Day*' peaked at an impressive, for the fifth single off the album, Number 10 when it was released at the end of May in 1988.

The single release from the album of '*So Emotional*' which gave Whitney another Top 5 British single was again overshadowed performance-wise with regards to the charts by the dizzy heights it would scale in America, where it became yet another Number 1 single on the Billboard charts, now her sixth in succession.

The album itself was more or less complete before the song had been recorded and subsequently added.

There were already ten tracks ready and completed but Clive Davis felt that the album needed one more song, especially an up-tempo one.

Enter Billy Steinberg and Tom Kelly, renowned American songwriters who had previously provided American Number 1's for Madonna, Cyndi Lauper and Heart with '*Like A Virgin*', '*True Colours*' and '*Alone*' respectively.

Kelly and Steinberg had not previously worked on any material with Whitney in mind and were perhaps more associated with the 'pop classic' style of writing, as so amply demonstrated by many of their songs that artists such as Madonna would subsequently record.

The song they would eventually come up with for Whitney's album, '*So Emotional*', began life with the working title of just plain, '*Emotional*' with the '*So*' being added later.

Steinberg and Kelly would later elaborate on their creative writing process together when Tom Kelly explained, "*Whenever we try to write a song for somebody, we usually end up writing something stupid and contrived, so it's best when we just write.*"

For the song *'So Emotional'* Kelly went on to explain how the sound began to evolve, saying, *"I started playing a bass line as we typically do with a drum computer and Billy had this lyric. It started off as a Prince type of thing, who's a real inspiration to us as being one of the few writers on the cutting edge, but as the song evolved we thought this would be good for Whitney."*

The song was then sent to Clive Davis who approved it as being suitable for Whitney's album and as being exactly what they were looking for and so the process of actually recording it began.

Narada Michael Walden was again in charge of production duties and spent two days at his studio in California putting the song together before flying to New York to record the vocals with Whitney.

The performance and the nature of the song were both good enough to have it included on Whitney's second album and the resulting decision to release the track as a single an excellent one as the song became yet another American Number 1 for Whitney, spending a week there in January of 1988.

The American record for the most consecutive Number 1 singles on the Billboard singles chart was achieved by Whitney with the release and chart topping performance of *'Where Do Broken Hearts Go'* in April, 1988.

Previously, both The Beatles and The Bee Gees had six consecutive Number 1 singles in America, but neither had been able to manage a seventh, something Whitney achieved, which was a momentous occasion that is probably unlikely to be equalled for many years to come, if indeed ever.

The record was achieved with the help of a different duo of songwriters for Whitney, having not been previously used, Frank Wildhorn and Chuck Jackson.

Frank Wildhorn had become aware of Whitney's blossoming voice and talents as far back as 1984 when he first heard her singing with Teddy Pendergrass on their duet, *'Hold Me'*. He was driving, together with his wife Rebecca in their car and he said to her at the time, *"That's a voice I would like to write for."*

His wish was to be granted when the song *'Where Do Broken Hearts Go'* was chosen as one of those for the new album and perhaps there's a bonus involved as well, being the song that broke the record for the most consecutive Number 1's in America.

Whitney's mind-blowing achievement in securing her seventh consecutive American Number 1 drew widespread praise from all corners of the world, with many previous critics and detractors now openly praising her incredible run of uninterrupted success.

Producer Narada Michael Walden summed up her achievement in his own unique style of praise and in equally mind-boggling fashion by declaring that, *"Whitney's seventh Number 1 in a row is not only a great achievement in the outer world but a most significant achievement in the inner worlds as well. There are seven lower worlds and seven higher worlds, with Whitney's seventh in a row, she takes us all to that seventh higher world. This is the place that all broken hearts go to for inner nourishment, inner satisfaction, inner and outer peace."*

The majority of the album's singles were contained within its first side whereas a more restrained, late night listening kind of mode was to be found on side 2. In commercial terms, some of side 2's material such as *'Where Are You'* and the pop driven feel of *'Love Is A Contact Sport'*, were weaker songs in regards to their potential hit status and yet despite this, they still were able to retain enough good rhythms and commercial sensibility to fit in neatly with the stronger sounding songs of the album as a whole.

Side 2 however, was not without its own potential show stoppers and chart toppers, particularly the song *'You're Still My Man'*. Written by the much respected and immensely sought after song-writing partnership of Michael Masser and Gerry Goffin, *'You're Still My Man'* was very much the potential chart topper that in fact never was.

Michael Masser and Gerry Goffin who had previously helped to take Whitney to the top of the charts with *'Saving All My Love For You'*, were again responsible for the words and music of *'You're Still My Man'*, which although it was never given the single status that perhaps it deserved, still remains one of Whitney's most popular tracks to this day and in its album form is always a staple on late night easy listening radio shows and is often requested on any such similar show. As is also *'For The Love Of You'*, co-written by members of erstwhile staples of the late night smooch music scene The Isley Brothers, who themselves have enjoyed a large degree of both singles and albums success throughout the world over a period of three decades now, initially going as far back as the sixties for their first major hit single, *'This Old Heart Of Mine'* and coming more up to date with songs as the still much covered *'Harvest For The World'*.

As if it actually needed it, the album went out anyway on another particularly exceptional high and with a real treat for Whitney's fans, the long hoped for duet with her mother Cissy Houston. For this momentous occasion they had obviously decided that it would require both a special song and a special performance. Fortunately they got it just right. Choosing to cover the show-stopping number from successful 1980's musical *'Chess'*, *'I Know Him So Well'* which had already been a chart topper in Britain courtesy of Elaine Page and Barbara Dickson who effortlessly took the song to the top of the British charts in February of 1984 where it remained for four weeks.

'I Know Him So Well' was a perfectly orchestrated finale to the album. A strong and confident vocal performance by both singers in which their vocals were perfectly inter-twinned around the song's intricate harmony parts, making for an undoubted highlight and the near perfect way to conclude the album.

Whitney and Cissy Houston's performance of the song was considered by many good enough to become a chart topper in its own right and although it was never released as a single many listed it as their particular highlight of what had been an accomplished and polished second album from Whitney.

And so in retrospect, any fears of suggestions that had floated around along the lines of Whitney being a flash in the pan who would not be able to keep up the consistently high standards of the first album, were soon dispelled and many critics began to accept that not only was Whitney immensely talented and had a clever and strong team behind her but that she was also going to be around for a long time to come yet.

Hitting back

After the completion of the second album and having undertaken the countless promotional and torturing obligations that accompanied it, Whitney was able to sit back and reflect on the enormity of what she had achieved in a career that had barely started and yet was more incredibly impressive already than many artists could ever dream of.

She was able to spend the time after the completion of the second album taking stock of her life and arranging among other things the move into her newly built house in Medham, New Jersey.

Everything seemed perfect in her life, all except that is, the constant barraging and complaints that were being thrown at her from persistent journalists. All of whom were looking for some sort of new story or angle to spread about where Whitney was concerned.

The latest in a long line of successive jibes was the criticism being levelled at her that her music was not representative of what or who she was. Too pop. Too white. Too bland, screamed headline after headline. Whitney appeared to take most of this in her stride until the subject of 'Too White' came up. Feeling threatened by this she felt she needed to answer back to this particular criticism. And that, she certainly did.

Soon after the event she was to be found speaking out on this subject. She was to proclaim that, *"Again and again I heard that I was too white. Because I had such huge success, I was accused of selling out, of being a black singer doing pop for white audiences". "I don't categorise either music or people on the basis of their colour. And there's no way I would attempt to make myself less black, whatever that entails, to be more commercial. I'm comfortable with myself and I don't want to change anything. I stay close to my roots. I don't pretend to be anything other than what I am - nor do I want to be. But for so long we've been tortured with this image problem - it used to be that if you wanted to sell records as a black artist, you didn't put your face on the sleeve. I'm not saying there's anything wrong with anyone who chooses to change their look for those reasons... but I don't want to sell out and I don't have the need to."*

'One moment in time'

The three year gap between the 'Whitney' album and her third, which arrived in 1990 and was provocatively titled 'I'm Your Baby Tonight' was a quiet and yet still productive part of her career for Whitney.

In September of 1988, another single was released but not from any of the previous albums.

'One Moment In Time' was written around and intended to inspire the United States of America Olympic team who would be competing in the games at Barcelona, Spain in 1990.

The video accompanying the song showed a succession of images of American athletes from the past and present, reaching new heights and goals, going faster, jumping higher and gaining near immortal greatness for their achievements. The style of the song very much reflected that too.

Whitney had, of course, nurtured her talents over the years for producing the big show stopping ballad that would inevitably bring the house down when she sang 'live' in concert and this song very much echoed that part of her repertoire at the same time as taking it on a further stage.

The sheer power and dramatisation of the lyrics that Whitney achieved in her performance of the song was enough for many to comment that she had another certainty for the Number 1 position in the charts on her hands and that it was merely a case of how long it would actually take to get there.

In reality the answer to that was not very long at all. 'One Moment In Time' became an expected British chart topper for two weeks during its eventual twelve week chart duration in the late summer of 1988.

As well as also reaching Number 1 on the singles charts of many other countries including Canada, Australia and Germany it was also yet another American Number 1 for Whitney, thereby continuing her remarkable record breaking achievements.

A year after *'One Moment In Time'* and Whitney was again a visitor to the charts, this time courtesy of a duet with long-time confidant and close family friend Aretha Franklin. Together they recorded the duet pop/R & B tinged number, *'It isn't, It wasn't, It ain't Ever Gonna Be'*.

Chart-wise, the song was something of a disappointment for the two because it only managed to reach Number 29 in theBritish charts. But the song was a bigger success in other ways, being a fine pairing of the two great singers and something of a special treat for the fans.

"There was a time when I first hit the scene that it was like I was on fire or something. For three years I was everywhere - I kind of got sick of myself in the end, and that's why I took a break after the second album. I couldn't take it any more. It got to the point where I'd lay down at night and I could feel people talking about me. In the end I had to get out of that fame aura for a while."

(Whitney Houston - The Times newspaper, 1992).

*"'I'M YOUR BABY TONIGHT' IS THE
DEFINITIVE 90's MORE BLACK POP RECORD.
WHITNEY WILL ALWAYS BE THE
SUPERSTAR NEXT DOOR."*

(Sounds Magazine)

*"THIS WILL SELL BY THE
TRUCKLOAD AND YIELD AT
LEAST FIVE HIT SINGLES."*

(Echoes Magazine)

"EVEN MORE ME-PLATINUM AWAITS"

(Select - Magazine)

"EXPECT ANOTHER MILLION-SELLER".

(Music Week)

*"SHOWCASES THOSE SUPERB VOCAL
CHORDS - AND, LET'S FACE IT,
THE LADY CAN SING!"*

(Blues & Soul Magazine)

*"'I'M YOUR BABY TONIGHT' IS AN
INTERESTING, CREDIBLE POP-DANCE
ALBUM. SUSPEND YOUR PREJUDICES
AND GIVE IT A LISTEN!"*

(M8 Magazine)

'I'm Your Baby Tonight' album

Despite some of the words taken from the reviews for the album 'I'm Your Baby Tonight' listed on the previous page, Whitney's third album was always going to be something of a tricky project to approach.

She was by now well and truly established as being one of the true great singing stars of the eighties and her phenomenal past track record was always going to be something that was somewhat difficult to live up to.

Most artists and singers, whoever they are, have traditionally had trouble with their third or 'difficult' albums, as they have come to be known. With the majority, it's merely a case of having used up most of the material to which they were signed to record or publish in the first place, and with Whitney, although she wasn't actually writing her own material, the choices that would have to be made as to what to tackle on this album were to become vitally important.

By now, Whitney was well and truly and perhaps slightly over emphatically placed within her own category of music. Known for her power ballads and credible and sensible pop tunes, the choice had to be made as to whether to continue down this particular road in the same vein or whether to take Whitney off at something of a tangent and try something new.

Of course, the public, on pretty much a world wide-basis, had been eagerly devouring anything and everything that Whitney delivered to them but there was a slight element of danger creeping in as to whether or not they would in fact still want more of the same. Her relentlessly smooth and sophisticated brand of music had, over the previous five or so years, taken the world by storm and she was somewhat pigeon-holed by her material.

This however, was not to deter either the lady herself or her particularly astute band of advisors when it eventually came to choosing new material for her third album.

In the end, 'I'm Your Baby Tonight' was to retain plenty of the undeniable distinctions that told the listener that this was a Whitney Houston album and yet it still managed to come up with a few surprises and risk taking faculties along the way.

One of the more evident changes was with regards to the personnel involved with helping to mould and construct the album's music. One of the biggest changes was to bring in the 'hot' and much in demand production team of L.A. Reid and Babyface, two much touted and respected figures in the American soul and R & B scenes.

Antonio 'L.A.' Reid and Kenny 'Babyface' Edmonds had a long list of credentials to their respective names by this time and were very much in demand throughout the world having previously worked with such successful acts as Bobby Brown, Pebbles, Karyn White and The Whispers, who Reid and Babyface had taken into the top 10 of the American singles chart with their song *"Rock Steady"*, which the pair had both written and produced for the group.

They were also no strangers to being members of various groups in the past years and enjoyed degrees of success on their own merits. In 1984, as members of the group The Deele they were to make their first impression on the American singles chart with the song *'Body Talk'* and four years later, in 1988, were to make their first inroads into the American Top 10 due to the success of the track *'Two Occasions'*. In the interim period, Babyface had written the song *'Slow Jam'* for the group Midnight Star and the two as a pair had also gained another American Top 10 single courtesy of the group The Whispers for whom they both wrote and produced the track *'Rock Steady'*.

It would be with Whitney Houston, however, that the pair would eventually achieve the distinction of having worked on both writing and producing an American Number 1 single.

Because of their long and distinguished line of writing and

production credits for other artists, Clive Davis felt that L.A. Reid and Babyface would be the perfect pairing to put Whitney with and help her come up with a slightly new and more distinctive harder edged sound for the new album.

There was a degree of criticism in some quarters by the press that the decision to have Whitney working with the team of L.A. Reid and Babyface on the new album was merely a ploy to gain her more respect and credibility from the black radio stations and audiences who had not been altogether supportive of some of her material in the past.

Whitney herself was to counter and answer these criticisms when being interviewed by the USA Today newspaper when she said, *"I would rather say to people that this new album is not different, it's just an extension of what Whitney has in store for them. I get flak just like everybody else, but I'm just doing what I do best. I didn't plan on what has happened in the past, it just happened. (Referring to the multi-million selling previous albums). I would think that black people would be proud, I don't sing music thinking this is black, or this is white, I just sing songs that I think and hope that everybody is going to like."*

L.A. Reid and Babyface had not met Whitney prior to working with her but they had written some of the songs that would eventually find their way onto the album, most notably the song that would become its distinctive title track, *'I'm Your Baby Tonight'*. Reid would later say of this, *"We wrote 'I'm Your Baby Tonight' among some other songs and when we felt we had something we asked her to come and see us in Atlanta. We met with her and had dinner, played the song for her and she was very happy."* Describing how they came up with the song, Reid would also later say that he felt it was, *"sort of a cross between something that's a little jazzy and a little funky which we thought would be ideal for her."*

Soon after L.A. Reid and Babyface had finished recording the basic structure of the song, it was ready for Whitney to come in and record the vocals, which were done in a relatively short period of time. The two were later to discover much to their approval that the song was not only definitely going to be included on the album but that even better, the record company had decided that it would become the title song. Reid explained his approval of this by saying, *"almost immediately after finishing once all the material had been recorded it was pretty much decided that would be the title song even then. We got a call that said, 'Guess what? You not only have the first single but you got the title track as well!"*

One of the criticisms that had been levelled by the press was that the inclusion of the two on Whitney's new album was a marketing ploy. Reid had to say on the subject, *"We wanted to come up with something that was different from anything Whitney had sung in the past, so we approached it from that angle. We wanted to give her a new direction and to pick the music up from where we felt she was lacking. We did feel that she needed more of a black base."*

In America, the single version of *'I'm Your Baby Tonight'* was again another Number 1 single for Whitney, reaching the summit of the charts there just seven weeks after its release and taking her now impressive tally of American Number 1 singles to eight.

In Britain, although the single was unable to reach the same heights it had achieved in America, it was however again another big success for her, eventually peaking at Number 5 in the British singles chart during its five week run.

'I'm Your Baby Tonight'
The reviews...

Following the estimated worldwide sales of between 25 to 30 million for the two previous albums, Whitney was going to have to come up with something pretty spectacular to keep both the critics and the public happy. In retrospect, she probably succeeded better with the public this time than with the critics, many of whom it would appear had the knives and daggers out gunning for her blood long before actually seeing or hearing the album in question.

The reviews for 'I'm Your Baby Tonight' varied from good to fair to bad, although having now run through them all there appears to be no common thread linking the bad ones with regard to what they actually thought was wrong about the album in the first place.

In reality even many of the bad reviews that the album was to receive contained many begrudgingly complementary comments within them.

One of the album's better reviews however came from the normally distinctly critical, 'Q' magazine. Reviewer David Roberts spoke honestly and informatively when he began his review by nicely setting the tone and ear marking just what Whitney had actually achieved over the years when stating, *"At the age of 27, Whitney Houston has the world at her feet and a string of supremely impressive statistics to her name. This third album follows in the steps of a first LP which has made its mark as the best-selling solo debut album of all time, and a second which saw her become the first female artist ever to debut at Number 1 in the US album charts. Add to that her catalogue of worldwide hit singles and a record breaking seven consecutive Number*

1 hit singles in the States and you begin to appreciate the sheer popularity of this gospel trained cousin of Dionne Warwick." He went on, *"Listen to more than a few bars of this album's opening hit single title track and you swiftly begin to appreciate the absolute and utter professionalism which has been at the heart of Whitney Houston's success".*

On the musical side he was to say that, *"Her seemingly effortless range and phrasing turn an up-beat blubber of a tune into instantly seductive high class pop soul of the first order... there is no doubting that this album confirms her right to sit a top her own particular pile."*

Other reviews were far more critical. Hot Press magazine for one, which stated that, *"she's only partially convincing on the ballad anthems like 'All The Man That I Need', where she sounds like a girlish cheer-leader."* But it is this particularly, that begins to show up the enormous conflicting reviews. Other magazines such as M8 and Echoes were proclaiming this particular track as being one of the album's undoubted highlights. Echoes magazine said that the track *'All The Man That I Need'* was, *"also worth a mention being a showy wide-screen better worth flinging pans around the kitchen to."* Praise indeed, all be it somewhat bizarrely stated. Elsewhere in the Echoes Magazine review of the album the reviewer Adam Mattera states that *"the ballads and lush mid-tempo cuts are just anonymously efficient and could equally comfortably reside on sides by Natalie Cole, Mariah Carey, etc."* Mattera goes on to criticise the album on one level as being in his own opinion, *"vacuous and lightweight"*, but does concede in more general terms that, *"As a commercial prospect it's every bit as powerful and well oiled as the Harley Davidson on the cover, strategically split 50-50 between the smoochable and the boppable."*

Some songs do come in for a special mention as being notable but the reviewer appears to feel within a whole that despite Whitney being in, *"as fine vocal form as ever,"* ultimately, *"we can only dream of what could have been."*

M8 magazine which had also praised *'All The Man That I Need'* as being one of the album's stand-out tracks also gave the album a more favourable review than many others. Describing the album initially as, *"A pleasing mix of up-tempo swing-beat numbers and the kind of over-the-top ballad only Whitney can manage,"* they went on to proclaim, as well as the aforementioned *'All The Man That I Need'*, that the album's stand-out tracks were undoubtedly the title track itself and also *'My Name Is Not Susan'*, which interestingly was the track that many of the more negative reviews chose to vent their particular brand of criticism on. One of which was Blues & Soul magazine which would describe the song thus, *"the overall impact is less than stunning with a number of below par ballad outings à la, 'My Name Is Not Susan.'"*

Looking over the Blues & Soul magazine review of the album as a whole, this actually ranks as one of the most disappointing, in part due to the magazine's respected standing within the black music arena.

Blues & Soul magazine's main criticisms of the album as a whole somewhat centres around the large number of producers used, and whilst this is generally thought to be a good thing and is recognised as a bolder step forward than on previous albums, the reviewer tends to feel that the big name producers themselves, (L.A. Reid & Babyface, Narada Michael Walden, Luther Vandross, Michael Masser and Stevie Wonder), are not used to their full potential and so don't complement the album in the way that was obviously the intention from the outset.

The reviewer of said article writes, *"Frankly the new album is a disappointment despite, (or perhaps as a result of), some very heavy weight support. Five producer units and Whitney herself along with Ricky Minor provide the eleven cuts on display, but, despite the (afore-mentioned) big guns on production the overall impact is less than stunning."*

The review does go on to set aside the Sam Dee's penned *'Lover For Life'* as being one of the better tracks in their opinion, but again returns to a more critical approach when the review continues with, *"Adequate would best describe the Derek Bramble co-written 'I Belong To You', even Luther (Vandross's) written and produced contribution 'Who Do You Love' fails to get the adrenaline or the heart beating to effect. It would have been interesting had, say, Jam & Lewis been invited into the studio to see what they could conjure up. Instead, what we have here is a pretty one dimensional and less than entertaining set. Much of this seems to be somewhat bland and hugely predictable material which leaves the lady little scope for showcasing those superb vocal chords."*

Other less than favourable reviews of the album were conjured up in the form of NME magazine whose reviewer said, *"Whitney sings better than ever, but so what? The world knows she can do better than this."* And also trade publication Music Week's review which proclaimed that it was a pity that, *"such a truly soulful voice (should be) wasted on such soul-less material.*

Finally, another more positive review in which Paul Lester of the now defunct Sounds magazine writes, *"Whitney Houston is the finest female soul singer of her era. (On the album), the love songs are the strongest. Sam Dees' 'Lover For Life' is beautifully light of touch, whilst 'After We Make Love' is a real twinkler, roomy enough for Whitney to really open up and give the song her best."*

'I'm Your Baby Tonight'
The music...

The music contained within the 'I'm Your Baby Tonight' album is a contrast of collected emotions and styles, gelled together on some occasions better than others. One of the highlights however is on the album's first side, track 2 'My Name Is Not Susan'. In the song, Whitney portrays a character who has been having a bit of trouble with a male companion who has taken to mumbling the name of a previous girl friend, (Susan). Whitney's character knows of this and tells him in no uncertain terms to either stop doing this or to find alternative sleeping arrangements.

The song was written by Eric Foster White and produced and arranged for the album again by L.A. Reid and Babyface and is tackled by Whitney in suitably peeved style as the troubled partner of the story. Whitney pulls this off particularly well and the song is something of a put -down to those critics in the past who falsely claimed that the lady was lacking in the sense of humour depart-ment. She does in fact tackle the song's subject matter with a lot of self-depreciating humour and this is reflected by its uniqueness.

'My Name Is Not Susan' was one of the new tracks that again really benefited from having the talented production team of L.A. Reid and Babyface behind it. Their particular form of production technique allowed the music to play a fuller role than in many of Whitney's previous tracks, giving the songs a much funkier feel, possessing a harder beat and giving the music much more attitude.

Another difference from previous albums was the actual layout of the cover, particularly its photographs. For 'I'm Your Baby To-night', Whitney was pictured sitting on a motorcycle which had a nice touch thrown in as the number plate of it read 'Nippy', a long time nickname of hers and now also the monicker bestowed upon her own management and production company that her father ran on her behalf.

Shortly after the title track of *'I'm Your Baby Tonight'* had finished its chart run in Britain, another single was reving up and soon ready to go in the form of *'All The Man That I Need'*.

The song was actually written as far back as 1981 by Dean Pitchford and Michael Gore and was originally intended to be recorded by singer Linda Clifford, who herself had previously found success when contributing her version of another Pitchford and Gore song, *'Red Light'*, to the sound-track album from the movie, *'Fame'*.

Linda Clifford recorded her version of *'All The Man That I Need'* for inclusion on her album *'I'll Keep On Loving You'* and it was subsequently released as a single but failed to chart in any significant way.

It was also released in a different guise in 1982 by Sister Sledge in a duet form with singer David Simmons. Again, though, it failed to make a large impact on the Billboard singles chart but did make a reasonable showing on The Hot Soul Singles chart in America, reaching Number 45.

Dean Pitchford said of all these different versions of his song that people were making but that no one was really scoring a major success with, that, *"I figured that it was one of those songs that was going to get cut a number of times and not ever have its day."* Pitchford however was a close friend of Arista president Clive Davis and it was over a dinner with him that the subject of the song *'All The Man That I Need'* again came up. After a discussion between the two parties regarding the song, a demo version of it was sent to Clive Davis who was impressed with the song but felt they would be unable to do anything with it at that time as this was around the period that Whitney had just in fact finished recording her second album. Then came a long and agonising wait for Pitchford while Arista went about the task of marketing Whitney's second album and so of course this meant that any plans for a third were still some way off.

During this interim period, Pitchford's publishers received many requests from interested parties who wanted one of their acts to record the song. The long wait proved to be fruitful however in the end when Whitney finally recorded it, with producer Narada Michael Walden again at the controls, and the song became Whitney's ninth American chart topper in February of 1991.

'All The Man That I Need' became a Number 13 hit in Britain when it was released during the notoriously difficult period of the British charts at Christmas, when practically all the singles, whatever they are, tend to stagnate somewhat for a period of two or three weeks and there is often little or no change with regards to chart positions. This is reflected by the song spending ten weeks on the British charts and yet not climbing any higher than Number 13, compared with the previous single, the *'I'm Your Baby Tonight'* title track which got as high as Number 5 despite spending just eight weeks in total on the charts.

Some reviewers actually thought the song was going to be a sure fire Number 1, the Melody Maker magazine review in Britain reading, *"this really ought to be Number 1 all over the world by Christmas."*

The reviews for the single in Britain again varied enormously. For example, in the Blues & Soul magazine it wasn't in fact the single's A side *'All The Man That I Need'*, that drew the praise this time, but the B side, a new track, previously un-released with the title, *'Dancing On The Smooth Edge'*. Blues & Soul gave the A side of the single something of a thumbs down verdict but were distinctly more impressed with *'Dancing On The Smooth Edge'*, calling the song, *"A major finding of form for the aspiring movie starlet, a cracking groove easing along with some beautifully light touches from Whitney and her backing vocalists."*

Elsewhere on the *'I'm Your Baby Tonight'* album, Whitney conjured up her usual range of vocals and passionate performances on the remainder of the album's tracks.

On the Sam Dees song *'Lover For Life'*, which was again produced and arranged by Narada Michael Walden, brought in again on this album to help add his distinctive production values to the Whitney sound, she was sure and yet authoritative on a song very much reminiscent of the kind of mid-tempo soul records now championed and explored so effectively by the likes of Lisa Stansfield and Mariah Carey.

'Lover For Life' was followed on the album by another of the

new L.A. Reid and Babyface written and produced numbers, *'Anymore'*. This was very much in the vein of being another harder hitting and dance orientated track that rather overawed and dominated the album's sound far more than on either of the previous two.

'Anymore' was a great success for Whitney in that both the music and more importantly her vocal performance seemed to have been given much more leeway and a far greater freedom than ever before and as a result were resplendent in their new found roles of freedom, testing her vocal capacities and bringing up new possibilities for what her voice could achieve in the future.

Side 2 of the *'I'm Your Baby Tonight'* album kicked off with *'Miracle'*, a L.A. and Babyface song that was to highlight the fact that not only were they accomplished writers of more up-tempo dance orientated songs but that they were equally as comfortable at producing the mellower and smoother type of material that Whitney had been so successful with in the past. *'Miracle'* did sound very much as though it would have sat comfortably alongside any of the material found on the previous two albums, being a far more restrained and reserved sounding track, fitting in comfortably enough with the general feel of this album but at the same time set aside from where the album's sound was generally heading.

Another song very much in the same style and mould as *'Miracle'* was *'I Belong To You'*. This song was in fact perhaps a little too laid back in its approach and interestingly was the first Whitney track, when released as a single from one of the albums, in many years to fail to make any sort of significant impact on the charts, only reaching a disappointing Number 54 in September of 1991.

The song *'I Belong To You'* was more of a success, however, in the context of the overall sound of the album itself, with a change of producer from the previous track of *'Miracle'* and yet still maintaining the general feel and mood created by its predecessor.

The relative failure of chart performance of *'I Belong To You'* when released as a single somewhat illustrated the comparable failure of the *'I'm Your Baby Tonight'* album project as a whole. Failure, is quite possibly far to strong a word to use in this context as the album has, in fact, so far notched up worldwide sales in excess of five million copies to date, a figure that will no doubt continue to grow even higher than that over the coming years. But when this is compared to the performance of the first two Whitney Houston albums, then there is indeed a relative disappointment where the album is concerned.

As a whole, the album did not contain an enormous chart topping single as the previous 'Whitney' and 'Whitney Houston' albums had with songs such as 'Saving All My Love For You' and 'I Wanna Dance With Somebody (Who Loves Me)'.

The songs that the album did contain would have comfortably graced many other artists' albums and consequently been accepted as being a major achievement. With Whitney, however, by this time, something spectacular was always expected wherever she was involved and this pressure seems to have manifested itself on this album.

The 'I'm Your baby Tonight' album had been Whitney's first major gamble within her carefully structured career pattern. Many just couldn't cope with the diversions she took within the musical content of the album and as an effect of this, dismissed the album as merely being Whitney's first major failure. This, though, was not really the case as the album, although compared with the previous two was not such a large seller, still maintained her position at the top of her profession.

Even those who dismissed the album as a whole still were able to fine one track or another on which to comment, 'Yeah, that's classic Whitney' and this all amounted in the end to the divisions within the public's choice.

Part two

Whitney on tour
1991...

Following on from the slightly disappointing reactions from some quarters to the *'I'm Your Baby Tonight'* project, Whitney set about seducing her audience once more from a different angle by going out and playing 'live' to tens of thousands night after night around the world.

Whitney's career was at this stage hardly flagging although she needed a boost and a show of support from her adoring public, going out and playing live to them was to be the perfect solution. Initially, however, the tour was beset by a series of unpredictable setbacks not least of which was the cancellation and temporary postponement of the whole of the European tour at one point due to the ever escalating events at the time, that were taking place in the Middle East, the Gulf War.

Whitney had been due to undertake a total of eighteen British dates which helped to form part of a larger scale European tour which would also be taking in Germany and Scandinavia amongst other countries along the way.

The eighteen date UK leg of the tour which originally had been planned to take place during March and April was reluctantly put back on her behalf because of the justifiable worries and reservations of travelling in and around Europe whilst the Gulf War raged. Many other performers were forced to cancel trips and subsequent tours in a situation that was also to affect businessmen and holiday makers as well to decide that to make the trip during these troubled times was a distinctly undesirable proposition.

John Houston, Whitney's father and the head of her company, Nippy Incorporated, which arranged the tour, issued a statement on the performer's behalf saying that, *"After much deliberation our concerns for the safety of the entire touring company could not be overcome and therefore became the prevailing factor in our decision to postpone the tour at this stage, regretfully, for the time being."*

The tour was rescheduled to take place starting in late August and running through September of 1991 instead and thankfully this time everything was able to run ahead as planned.

The Star Spangled Banner...

As something of a compensatory factor to the fans immensely disappointed by this news and as a result of the literally huge public demand for the single it was eventually released in the UK.

Originally, however, there had been no plans at all for the single to be granted any kind of worldwide release, the record company feeling that it would not appeal so much to a large scale audience due to its particular patriotic meaning to the American people. A spokesperson quipped at the time about the initial decision to release it just in America that it would only appeal to them and they would not expect British people to want to buy it in the same way, saying that, *"would you expect the Americans to want to buy Betty Boo singing 'God Save The Queen'"*. Although in retrospect, Betty Boo tackling the Sex Pistols' version of the song could well have proved to be an interesting proposition.

Whitney's eventual version of *'The Star Spangled Banner'* again proved a wise choice of material for her when its commercial release was accompanied by the usual series of record breaking feats. Her version of the song which was to eventually top the American charts was primarily taken from a live rendition of the song that she gave at the American football's 'Super Bowl' championships of January 27th, 1991.

Whitney was following in some distinguished footsteps when taking on the honour of singing the National Anthem at the Super Bowl. Previously, the task had been undertaken by the likes of

Diana Ross and Billy Joel, but Whitney's performance of the Anthem was considered one of the most emotive which was to lead to its subsequent release as a bona fide recording of the event.

It was suggested and rumoured that the song was not a complete 'live' rendition of the song she sang at the Super Bowl but that it was in fact a combination of both this version and a subsequently recorded studio version of the song that were gelled together in order to produce the final result. Whatever, the outcome proved to be as spectacular as one had come to expect from a Whitney Houston recording and the public soon bought the record in their droves.

'The Star Spangled Banner' had actually started life as a poem by Francis Scott Key and was written during the British attack on the area of Fort McHenry in Baltimore during 1814. The poem was originally given the title of 'Defence Of Fort McHenry' in order to represent this time in American history.

Although there is no precise date for when it may have occurred, the poem was only set to music many years later for the song 'To Anacreon In Heaven', thought to be written by John Stafford Smith, who was in fact a British composer.

Although this interpretation of the song had been used by the American military service since 1916 it was not officially adopted as such for the national anthem of America until around 1931 when it became recognised on a more wide spread basis and became their official National Anthem.

Consequently, over the years, the song has been recorded in hundreds of different versions, some timeless classic, others, 'unique'. A couple of the more famous versions of 'The Star Spangled Banner' were provided by Jimi Hendrix and TV comedy actress Roseanne Barr respectively. Hendrix's version often found on his 'live' recordings of both official release and bootleg albums was a typical *tour de force* of raw guitars fuelled with emotion whilst Roseanne's was a hysterical version that she sang and which was dismissed by US president George Bush as being, *"a national disgrace."*

Whitney Houston's version of the song was released in America in the wake of the Gulf War and its patriotic leanings were a huge boost towards its subsequent popularity there and this was very much reflected in its chart and sales performances, particularly initially sales-wise where it was to sell over a million copies within a fortnight.

Whitney's version of *'The Star Spangled Banner'* proved such a hit in fact, that it became at the time the fastest selling single in America since the charity recording *'We Are The World'*, the American counterpart of the Live Aid inspired, Band Aid group recorded *'Do They Know It's Christmas (Feed The World)'* in 1985.

The song was also to break new ground in America for Whitney in another respect by becoming her highest first week chart entry so far when it crashed onto the Billboard charts there after its first week of release at Number 32. Her previous highest entry in America had been when *'I Wanna Dance With Somebody (Who Loves Me)'* entered the chart some six places lower at Number 38 in 1987.

Around the same time that Whitney's version of *'The Star Spangled Banner'* was being prepared for its release, Whitney was the recipient of yet another award to add to her already immensely impressive collection. She was named American Musical Performer Of The Year at the 8th Annual American Cinema Awards and was again in distinguished company with, among other nominated who also received awards for work in their respective fields, actors James Stewart, Tom Cruise and Lauren Bacall.

*"WHITNEY'S DISH OF THE DAY
CERTAINLY HAD ALL THE INGREDIENTS
FOR AN EVENING'S ENTERTAINMENT
THAT FEW OF HER CONTEMPORARIES
COULD RIVAL".*

(Blues & Soul magazine).

*"A VOICE OF LIQUID GOLD WHICH
SHE USES TO MAXIMUM EFFECT...
THE RANGE IS FANTASTIC."*

(Daily Mail)

WHITNEY LIVE...

*"EACH TIME SHE SEEMED TO
HAVE PEAKED HER VOICE
SOARED AGAIN TO REACH NEW
AND PASSIONATE HEIGHTS."*

(Daily Telegraph)

*"WONDERFUL WHITNEY SHONE BRIGHTER
THAN HER SEQUINED OUTFITS."*

(Daily Express)

*"HOUSTON LEAVES THE STAGE WITH HER
ARMS ALOFT, A GESTURE MORE FAMILIAR
FROM WOMEN'S ATHLETICS THAN POP,
ALTHOUGH THAT MIGHT BE APPROPRIATE...
...THE SHOW IS A MEDAL WINNER."*

(The Independent)

Whitney 'live'
What the critics said...

Following the initial disappointment when the originally planned concerts had to be cancelled, it was considered a general relief all around when it became clear that Whitney most certainly would be arriving in the UK in late August for her concerts which were primarily to take place during the month of September.

Whitney's eighteen British concerts, taking in London, Birmingham and Glasgow were to form part of a gruelling World Tour that would be scheduled to last for well over a year and visit many countries around the world where Whitney had yet to appear 'live'.

Everything seemed to be running smoothly for the British leg of the concerts but behind the scenes there was trouble brewing. Not for Whitney especially or any of her entourage, but for many of the fans who had attempted to buy tickets for the concerts and had unwittingly become the victims of a huge concert ticket scam that was occurring at the time.

The scam involved a Leicester based company who went under the name of Mercer Promotions Limited. The company had taken out a large number of advertising spaces in many publications including national newspapers and offered concert tickets not just for the Whitney Houston concerts but also for other big box office draws of the time such as New Kids On The Block, John Denver and Deacon Blue, all of whom were either undertaking or planning to start major British concert tours at the time.

All in all the fans who had attempted to buy tickets from the company had lost an estimated £50,000 between them and it was a dark shadow cast over what was otherwise a successful venture for Whitney.

The unfortunate fans who had sent off their hard earned money to this phoney company, who were using a Box Office number in the Beaumont Lees area of Leicester had not surprisingly had their cheques cashed but were to receive no tickets in return. The police were called in to investigate the matter and a detective on the case soon advised potential buyers not to send any more money orders or cheques to the bogus ticket sellers.

The Marshall Arts organisation who were promoting the British concerts on Whitney's behalf were naturally enough horrified by what had happened but had to reluctantly explain that there was little to nothing that they could personally do about the situation as the tickets supposedly being offered probably didn't exist in the first place.

Shortly after, a man was arrested and questioned about the matter with another warning being issued about the bogus tickets in order to try and prevent anyone else falling foul of the scheme.

Of course, this incident was not exclusively aimed towards Whitney as it invariably happens when any big name performer is about to undertake concerts and many unscrupulous individuals see a way of obtaining a fast buck, but it was a slight setback and a sour footnote to what had been a highly enjoyable series of concerts.

As for the concerts themselves, almost all the dates announced had in fact sold out in a very short period of time and subsequently tickets proved hard to come by . The touts did a roaring trade outside the venues with high prices being offered and the fans willing to pay more than double the face value of these tickets in order to get into the concerts and actually see Whitney performing in the flesh.

Reviews for the concerts, as so often is the case, varied wildly. For example David Cheal of The Daily Telegraph started his particular review with a niggle in the form of criticising the show's basic outlay and structure, saying, *"Great slices of her 90 minute show were padded out with the kind of sideshows which seem to constitute the bulk of so many concerts these days; introductions to the band, guest spots for backing singers, rap routines, dance routines, instrumental bits and just plain old patter."*

Despite this, he was to concede that Whitney herself was an undoubted star of the highest calibre and was more than able to *"deliver the goods 'live'"* as it were when he went on to write, *"But when she sang, she sang. Especially on the ballads. Her voice cruised majestically through a medley of love songs, including, 'Didn't We Almost Have It All' and 'Where Do Broken Hearts Go', showing that all the care lavished on the early stages of her career had borne fruit."*

Words of praise were also forthcoming from the reviewer's pen when he wrote of the ethics of actually staging the concert itself and set about exploring the concepts and motives behind what Whitney was attempting to portray and deliver in her 'live' performances. He wrote, *"The stop-start approach pursued by so many American artists seems to be a desire to inject 'showmanship' into their performances. The result often can be a lack of momentum. But it does also suggest a commitment to the concept of entertainment and this has its benefits, since it guarantees that the musicianship will be of the highest calibre and that the staging will be both bold and imaginative. All of this was certainly true of Whitney Houston's show. The musicianship was hard to fault and after disappearing to freshen up again Whitney emerged wearing her fourth costume of the evening to wind up the show with a ravishing finale. Each time she seemed to have reached her peak her voice soared again to reach new and passionate heights. It was worth waiting for."*

Another reviewer to attend the shows staged at London's Wembley Arena was Lester Middlehurst of The Daily Mail who again had much to praise about the show's content and the performance of the lady herself. He wrote, *"Like the gospel songs she delivers with such dynamic impact, Whitney Houston has got the whole world in her hands. Standing on the stage the 5 ft. 11 in. beauty is queen of all she surveys. Still only 28 she is secure in the knowledge of her own fame. She has never resorted to gimmicks to sell herself or her music. Not for her, Madonna's outrageous outfits and videos, the nude photo-spreads employed by La Toya Jackson or the public slanging matches popular with Cher. This cool, sophisticated lady commands the audience's attention and by the end of the night she has them joining in a gospel songs medley despite the fact, as she herself points out, that few of them have probably set foot inside a church."*

The reviewer also addressed the issue of just what a strong hold Whitney Houston is able to have over her audience when describing how, *"Like the superstar she is she tries (the audience's) patience. She is not afraid to walk off stage for one of her numerous costume changes or simply to take a break. But each return is greeted with even greater enthusiasm. Whitney employs a chameleon-like quality to keep her audience enthralled. One minute she is the disco queen, dressed in a figure-hugging sequined spangled cat suit as she belts out 'I Wanna Dance With Somebody', (the next minute), she switches her powerhouse voice to numbers like 'So Emotional' and 'Saving All My Love For You.'*

Plenty of praise indeed there from The Daily Mail's reviewer Lester Middlehurst, who was also quick to point out the important roles played by Whitney's band and back up performers on stage, particularly giving a mention to Whitney's four backing singers, *"each of whom could pursue a solo career"*, he stated.

Finishing off his review, Middlehurst wrote, *"For the fans Whitney can do no wrong. She knows it and she uses it. The queen of the music world."*

More praise, but with a degree of criticism as well were contained within other reviews. Giles Smith of The Independent newspaper appears, from much of the tone of his review, to have gone to the concert as something of a neutral outsider none too keen on what he was to witness and yet the over riding line of thought going through the review again suggests towards the end that he was to come away from the concert with a much higher and more respected opinion of Whitney's show than when he arrived. His review centres around one of the performances given by Whitney outside London, in fact at the somewhat cavernous NEC Arena in Birmingham.

He starts by setting the scene at the beginning of the concert in his own unique style by explaining Whitney's first foray onto the stage at the beginning of the show. He writes, *"Houston's band take the stage well ahead of her, her musical director conducting an introductory piece for synthesizer and wind instrument. It sounds like movie music but as it builds, it changes gear and becomes more akin to the theme music for a cop show. The lights begin to go up and flicker intensely.*

The smart money at this point is on an evening of shimmer and tinsel, but in fact, this is the last opportunity for camping it up that the band is going to get. They (the band) break abruptly into 'I Wanna Dance With Somebody'. Houston arrives late enough to be well inside the first verse as she comes. She walks on from the back, a modest entrance - at least as modest as you could manage if at the time you happen to be wearing a bright blue body-suit, dusted with glitter from head to toe. The voice cuts clear of the instrumentation straight away. It is marginally sharp for the first half-verse, but then it locks into pitch and stays there. Houston goes at the song from an angle which will have surprised those expecting risk-free renderings of the versions familiar from the records. She cuts the lines up, re-phrases them and threads new loops through the melodies."

Smith went on later in the review to again praise the choice of arrangement, reflected in the delivery by Whitney given to many of the songs, particularly the older familiar ones when he wrote, *"The show slows for 'Saving All My Love For You'. Again Houston chips away at the familiar melody. On record the song is the aural equivalent of a poster with kittens on it. Done live, (however), it suddenly has drama. Similar things happen to 'Didn't We Almost Have It All' and 'Where Do Broken Hearts Go' revealing how the soapy production of her albums can sap the potency of her voice. 'The Greatest Love Of All', played for an encore, could easily have arrived as a tiresome piece of cheermongering, but not when worked at like this."*

These sentiments were echoed by the review giving to the concert by Michael Soyannwo in respected black music publication Blues & Soul magazine.

His review had started in derogatory style but again had changed course during the article in order to reflect the genuine surprise that many had obviously experienced, particularly when witnessing a Whitney Houston concert for the first time.

The review often levelled criticism at Whitney and her music, that her choice of material was not always considered desirable or appropriate for a black audience and that the music was too blatantly aimed at a white main stream one. He said, *"Houston's place in black music has often been questioned amongst those who consider her music far too commercial or 'white' to ever be ranked alongside a truly 'black' artist such as Aretha Franklin. I'm sure many of those critics smiled knowingly when Whitney opened her show with 'I Wanna Dance With Somebody' and littered much of her set with 'pop standards'. However, what came in between may well have persuaded some of these people to think again. She excelled vocally when performing ballads such as 'Saving All My Love For You' and 'All The Man That I Need', which clearly demonstrated why Whitney Houston is the biggest selling black female artist around at the moment and will probably continue to be so throughout the nineties."*

Finally on the review side of the concerts, Annie Leask of The Daily Express was none too impressed with the stage sets or the dance troupe, calling the latter *"sluggish"*, and the sets, *"disappointingly dull"*, but she too seemed more than amply compensated for what were in her opinion these shortcomings when it came to analysing the more important factors of the performance, especially that of Whitney's vocals. On this subject the reviewer was again complimentary in her praise saying that, in particular, *"Her performance of 'Revelation' was almost a religious experience and the enthralled Wembley Arena crowd rose to its feet."* She too seemed more than impressed by the show's grand finale saying, *"Whitney closed the 90 minute show by giving full range to a voice that could fill a cathedral unaided in an emotional encore of 'The Greatest Love Of All'. The soul star once again proved that she is very much a class act."*

So all in all the reviewers, many of whom appeared to approach the idea of having to review the concerts with a large degree of trepidation all seemed pretty much unanimous in the end to the fact that they were indeed witnesses to one of the 'live' highlights of the year and that Whitney Houston was a performer who could more than ably hold her own when it came to performing 'live' to an audience.

Whitney on...

(Whitney herself quoted over the years on a variety of different subjects).

DIONNE WARWICK

Whitney says, "*I always used to look up to her as a little girl and would often spend a lot of time either with or around her. I always admired and respected her so much because whatever the situation she (Dionne) would always hold herself with such charm and grace. To me she was always the perfect model of someone who survived within the music business and was able to do it in such a dignified way. Spending so much time with her when I was younger taught me an awful lot and I think the three best words to describe Dionne are grace, charm and talent.*"

It was always a long standing expected engagement that once Whitney had established herself within the music business that she should inevitably record a duet with Dionne Warwick. However, the two of them never saw it as clearly as some people would have liked them to.

They did, however, come together as a musical *tour-de force*, particularly around the time that Dionne was heavily involved in her work at promoting Aids awareness and helping to stage benefit concerts around the United States.

Of the expected collaboration between the two of them, Dionne herself has said, "*The first time that Whitney and I finally found a song that we felt we wanted to sing together was when we knew it would be right. Obviously everyone had expected and anticipated from the very outset of Whitney's career that we would do something together, but we were almost simultaneously saying that when the right song happens, that's when we'll do it. We certainly had no intention of just going in to record any old song together just for the sake of it just because we are related. It had to be something that both of us felt happy about, we always say now that we will record a song together if we both feel it's a good enough tune."*

STEVIE WONDER.

"Stevie's great! He calls me at any hour because he never seems to have any idea what time it is. He once sang to me on the phone at six o'clock in the morning, a new song he had written with me in mind. Next thing he faxed the lyrics over and we recorded the duet together.

GOD

"I've always kept God as my head and that way I can't get above God and I don't want to be bigger than he is. Having God in my life creates a mildness and meekness in your soul and in your heart that you can't escape. So if you remember those things it helps. My family, for example, especially my mother always inject that into me all the time. It's that that helps to keep me sane. I know I can make big money and go to all these fabulous places and do all these things but at the end of the day God still stays the same and is still there."

CISSY HOUSTON

"My mother is the only one who I'll go sit on her lap and ask, Mum, do you know what am I going to do or how am I going to do this or that, but that's my mother you know. Even at the age I am now I still feel the need to and am able on occasions to go and literally sit on her lap and seek help and guidance if I need to and just say, Mum I've got a problem or Mum listen to this, and so I can run any ideas I may have by her and I feel there are many times when you can only go to your mother for that kind of help and support.

But you know for the most part I don't even have to do that because she's got such a strong connection with all her children that she will actually call me at the weirdest moments, the weirdest times and say,

"What's going on with you, I just dreamt about you last night and I know something's going on in your heart." And so we'll talk about it together and work it out. I always know she will be there for me whenever I need her help or support."

MADONNA

Whitney has been quoted as saying about Madonna that, *"I'd kill my kids if they grew up to look like her. She says nasty horrible things like you can go to bed with whoever you want, you can go to the trashiest clubs. She should have more responsibility to the children who buy her records and who gave her all she has today."*

She also does admit however on the subject of Madonna that she is also one of the smartest and most ambitious women in the music industry, but adds rather cheekily that she thinks that because Madonna is a Leo like herself.

THE RECORD INDUSTRY

"It's a nasty, nasty business. It's lowdown. A lot of the time it makes me feel like I want to get out. There's just so many different angles to it all now. These days you don't particularly have to be a very good singer, you don't have to be able to dance. You just have to have a nice body and a nice face and you're made. You often don't even have to go anywhere near a studio or be able to sing properly. It's that kind of thing I hate and it makes me think to myself, you know, where are we going, what are we doing and where's the real talent here? If you start tripping on it and believing the hype, you become a monster. And I don't want to become a monster, I want to be seen as being just a nice person."

ACTING

"I think it was kind of like a natural progression for me to make, to become a singer/actress. It's a different situation to become a singer when you're an actress and that's quite rare and more difficult to do. But for most singers its a natural thing for them I think. I mean you're interpreting songs and when you're on stage performing you're acting out the words anyway. So when you get to the stage of being in a movie you're doing something very similar. But what is different about the movies is the

actual speaking part and having to deliver the lines convincingly. I'm used to having to sing everything emotionally and that comes naturally enough, but making the transition is the harder part. That's the big difference between the two but for the most part it is in fact just a kind of natural progression."

PRIVACY

Whitney Houston's private life has, as practically everyone must be aware, always been the subject of intense media speculation and has resulted in many and various rumours being circulated over the years since she first hit the headlines in a big way and became a worldwide singing sensation. Prior to her marriage to singer Bobby Brown in the summer of 1992, it was almost impossible for any movement Whitney made in public to go unnoticed or unreported.

In the early days the press had a field day linking her with many and varied stars such as Robert De Niro and Eddie Murphy, always insisting that whoever she was seen with had some sort of ulterior motive attached to it.

Whitney herself seems to have reacted in public and during interviews to this gross invasion of her privacy over the years in surprisingly good spirit.

When talking about the problems she has faced over the years with this press intrusion she has said light-heartedly that, *"Yeah, I just read something the other day that said something like, 'Yeah she's married but you know she's having an affair with some woman or something, I don't know. But you know although I often laugh at these things it can be a bit de-moralising on occasion or degrading, you know."*

When talking during her early years about romantic liaisons, Whitney also went on to explain that she felt that, *"I've had boyfriends all my life, but I've never been one to have five at the same time. I was raised a Christian and my mother was very strict with me as far as boys were concerned. She told me that the way to a man's heart is not by sleeping with him at the drop of a hat. I believe in preserving myself because nobody likes anything that's old and worn out, I'm determined I'll save myself until the right man comes along and I'll know when that happens."*

WHY THE 'BODYGUARD' FOR HER ACTING DEBUT.

"The thing about it was that I just didn't want to do just any old film for the sake of it. I'd been sent scripts over the years but didn't feel that any of them were at all suitable. The one for 'The Bodyguard' came. I was determined that whatever I chose to do it would have to be something that 'added-up', not just be a case of, "oh, look, she did a film, how nice, Whitney's in the movies, etc." I mean it took me a while to find a script that I was happy with like 'The Bodyguard'.

I waited a long time for something like that to come along and I think that if I play my cards that way and am smart about what I chose to do not just doing anything for the sake of it then I can keep the momentum going. Besides, Hollywood's happy!"

THE LOS ANGELES RIOTS

Contrary to a great deal of widespread popular belief, it would seem that Whitney Houston is, in fact, very much aware of what is going on in the world around her, and when asked for an opinion or about her particular feelings on a subject, is often very vocal.

In an interview, Whitney was asked about how she had viewed the Los Angeles riots, that took place following the acquittal of the policemen accused in the Rodney King trial, she said, *"I can understand the anger. If you're talking about oppressed people who feel like they have no power, no hope, then sure. Of course there were those who were out there rioting for no particular reason but I can sympathise with people who have nothing and feel everything is working against them. It was a social earthquake - and in a lot of ways it was waiting to happen. There are a lot of people in Los Angeles who I think feel they have been forgotten and what happened was a way of being heard."*

Whitney Trivia

THE WHITNEY HOUSTON FACT FILE:

FULL NAME: Whitney Elizabeth Houston

DATE OF BIRTH/PLACE OF BIRTH: Whitney was born on the 9th August, 1963 in Newark, New Jersey.

STAR SIGN: Leo, the fiery sign represented by a Lion.

FAVOURITE FOOD: Chinese Fried Chicken, Macaroni Cheese. She also enjoys eating Sushi, Tomato soup and especially Peanut Butter and Jam sandwiches!

FAVOURITE DRINK: Piña Coladas (though Whitney says they must be well made and creamy).

FAVOURITE HOBBIES: Sleeping a lot! Playing Tennis, lifting weights, swimming and lazing around on the beach. Whitney says she also likes to relax by listening to Gospel music.

FAVOURITE HOLIDAY DESTINATION: The Caribbean, (and Whitney likes one island in particular, but she's keeping its name a firm secret).

FAVOURITE BOOK: Hollywood Wives by Jacky Collins.

FAVOURITE FILM: A Star Is Born

FAVOURITE ACTOR: Al Pacino

FAVOURITE ACTRESS: Jessica Lange

FAVOURITE COLOUR: Lavender

MOST FRIGHTENING EXPERIENCE: *"The first time I went on stage and sang a solo. My mother rang me up out of the blue, complaining that she was too busy to be able to do a show that was booked for her and asked if I would be able to do it instead. Only in retrospect I realise there was nothing wrong with her, and that she was only testing me, to see if I could manage to do something like that myself. I was scared to death about doing the show, but it turned out to be a great experience, to do my own show as it gave the confidence I needed for the future".*

HEALTH AND BEAUTY: Whitney says that she often has terrible trouble trying to keep her naturally curly hair under control and that at times it appears to have a will of its own!

To help combat this problem she will often wear wigs, although this can work out to be somewhat expensive as most of the ones she wears cost anything from between £200 to £600 each.

For her own hair though she uses a special concoction as a form of conditioner. This consists of mixing together a combination of cocoa butter and coconut oil which she massages into her scalp and will leave on for about half an hour while she enjoys a relaxing bath.

As for make up generally Whitney will use very little even whilst on stage, whenever possible.

This stems back to her childhood when she was forbidden by her parents from using make-up until she was sixteen years old. Because of this she says that she often still doesn't feel comfortable when wearing make-up, particularly lipstick, as it still makes her feel like she's doing something wrong. However, the time she spent as a model was very useful in her learning many 'tricks of the trade' where make-up is concerned, particularly how to make the most out of using very little.

On stage quite often the only make-up she will wear is a clear lip gloss and a touch of mascara and more often than not, none what so ever when off stage and just relaxing at home.

She maintains a strict beauty regime that consists of cleansing her skin twice daily with a moisturiser, but besides this it's very minimal .

In her earlier years she was teased by many of the other black girls at school because her skin colour was much lighter than many of theirs, and for a while this bothered her although she now says that that is all behind her and she's very happy with the colour of her skin.

PETS: Whitney absolutely adores animals and is particularly fond of her two cats Mister Blu and Marilyn.

She once spent £3000 on buying two specially made diamond encrusted collars for the cats, and her chef creates special meals for them to eat each day.

Another special extravagance for her animals was bestowed upon her two pedigree dogs, Lucy and Ethel, they live in a degree of luxury themselves as Whitney had special kennels worth £28,000 made for them.

Lucy and Ethel are Akidas, large dogs, slightly wolf-like in appearance with big manes. Whitney is especially fond of them because they were bought for her by Bobby Brown as a present during their engagement. Of the two dogs she says they help to remind her of Bobby when he's away and *"They comfort me when I'm alone."*

CARS: Whitney adores cars and they play a big part in her life.

When she first started out as a model her mode of transport was an old and battered four door Toyota.

Since she has made it big however she has been able to indulge in her passion for cars more vehemently.

Most impressive of all among her collection these days, and her favourites are her Mercedes 500 Sports, a Ferrari, and a Range Rover. She also owns a few other smaller cars, for more general and practical purposes.

DIETING: Whitney readily admits that at only 8 st. for her 5 ft. 11 in. height if anything she's slightly too skinny. But she admits that she carefully monitors whatever she eats and that if when she weighs herself she has gone above her eight stone ideal she'll diet to lose any excess pounds.

If it happens that she does go above her eight stone limit at any time then she'll take drastic action.

She'll undertake a strict regime where food is concerned and will place particular emphasis on eating a diet consisting mainly of fruit and vegetables. She says she also maintains a regimented work-out period in which she'll do a variety of aerobic type exercises with her personal fitness trainer.

MUSICAL CONTRIBUTIONS: As well as her own record break-ing solo achievements, Whitney has contributed in some form usually dueting with various other artists on their albums.

These include singing with Chaka Khan, Teddy Pendergrass, Jermaine Jackson, The Neville Brothers and Lou Rawls. She also recorded duets with both her mother Cissy Houston and her aunt Dionne Warwick.

Dionne Warwick says of her duet with Whitney that, *"people were constantly asking me when I was going to record a song with Whitney, and we both decided that it had to be the right song and that we shouldn't just do it for the sake of it, so it was a case of when that song came along we both knew it was the right time."*

CLOTHES: Whitney herself says, *"On stage I tend to wear shimmery dresses but off stage I prefer more casual clothes such as jeans and leather jackets. I always try to look clean, neat and classy. I had a strict upbringing and now I hate wearing plunging necklines. My stage clothes can cost more than £1,000 a dress. I love buying clothes and my favourite colour is probably lavender but most of my outfits tend to be black."*

WHOOPS!: One of Whitney's undoubted most embarrassing moments came on the nationally broadcast American Merv Griffin TV show. She was singing her American Number One single *'How Will I Know'* and everything appeared at the time to be going fine. However, she was wearing a skimpy top with rather loose straps. Whilst singing the song she was looking down at the members of the audience in the front few rows. She noticed that all of the men were sitting there somewhat goggle-eyed. She couldn't understand just what it was that was keeping them so glued to her and so amused until a helpful woman who caught her eye gestured to Whitney that one of her breasts had slipped out of her top and was on full few to the members of the audience. Rather embarrassed Whitney quickly re-adjusted herself and in true professional style carried on singing the song to its conclusion.

She does say however that she doesn't know how to this day that she didn't freeze on the spot and stop the recording and that although she carried on undaunted it was undoubtedly one of the most embarrassing moments of her career to date.

AWARDS: Whitney has of course over the years been honoured and has won many and varied awards.

Some of these have been well known and prestigious honours such as her Emmy, but others are less well documented and in one or two cases bizarre to say the least.

For example, two of her more strange awards consisted firstly of, 'Points of Light Contributing Leadership Award', which incidentally was presented to her by President George Bush, and her award from the American Dental Association, where she was honoured and given an award for having the 'Greatest American Smile'.

Among her impressive range of awards more recognisable on a world-wide level, she has won:

* **2** Grammy Awards
* **11** American Music Awards
* **5** People's Choice Awards
* **2** Emmy Awards

MODELLING: Whitney has said of her time as a model, which incidentally proved to be a lucrative period of her life in which she not only got her faced noticed in a lot of the right places but was also a cover girl for magazines such as Glamour and Seventeen magazine, that, *"I modelled because the money was good. I was totally caught off guard. My mom and I were in New York and this guy walked up to us in the street and said, "Do you model? You should, because you are tall, you are beautiful. You should go to this modelling agency because they are looking for someone like you". "So I went and they signed me up that day. Little did I know then how much money I'd be making. At one point I was working for only about two hours a day and was making five thousand dollars."*

WHITNEY'S TEENAGE YEARS: Whitney says, *"Cracking gum and sitting with your legs open was considered unacceptable. I wasn't allowed to wear make-up until I was 14 or date boys until I was 16.*

She continues, *"I went through what every teenager goes through I guess. I listened to what she said and then I just wanted to go the other way". "She said we want you to go to college so you don't turn out to be too much of a 'homegirl'. I didn't always listen and I moved out. But today I have to laugh and think, 'Mmm, maybe she was right'."*

CHILDHOOD DREAMS: One of Whitney's earliest desires and dreams was, of all the strange things, to become a Basketball player! She says, *"One of my secret ambitions has always been to play basketball but I never could. I never had that co-ordination. Both my brothers play but I love to see women athletes play because when guys play it's so fast I can hardly see the ball or what's going on."*

CHILDHOOD TRAUMA: Where Whitney grew up in the 1960's

was a particularly rough area of town and in a later interview she re-called how; *"I grew up in a pretty tough area first and then the riots took place in the '60s. I remember lying on the floor because bullets were flying. I grew up in the ghetto. After the riots my mother and father worked so hard to get us out of there and we moved to what was a better part of town."*

WHITNEY ON CHOOSING THE RIGHT SONG: Whitney has said on this subject; *"You know how I really know when a song is special? When I can take it and relate it to my human nature or my spiritual nature. For me I can relate it to my God. There is a love when you know the Lord or God for yourself that no man or human sprit can fulfil. It's a spiritual thing for me when choosing a song. It's coming from God. Which goes far deeper than the human love for me."*

WHITNEY'S PET NIGGLE: *"The one thing I hate about the music business is that so many things are said about you which aren't true. People take things out of context which aren't true. Things you say aren't repeated the same way. Also what annoys me is when people tell me things like, "I'll call you in an hour", and they never call. That aggravates me."*

WHITNEY ON RAP MUSIC: *"I like rap music but not all of it. I think some rap doesn't mean anything. I like artists like Ice T., Melle Mel, LL. Cool J, Heavy D... I really haven't gotten into NWA though. All that stuff about the negative being as great as the positive. They're making money out of controversy, which I don't think I necessarily agree with."*

WHITNEY'S VIEW ON THE PROBLEM OF AIDS: *"Aids is not something that is discriminating. It is not just homosexuals. It is babies. It is children. It is mothers. It is fathers. It is daughters. It is sons. It is everybody. Let's get real here. It is not just one person's problem. It is everybody's problem."*

WHITNEY ON THE TABLOID PRESS: Whitney has said in the past of being hassled by the tabloid press that; *"At first, I used to get hurt by it because, apparently, people knew more about me than I knew about myself! But you do sort of become used to it."*

WHITNEY ON CHILDREN: In an interview given before becoming pregnant and subsequently giving birth to daughter Bobbi,

Whitney said; *"My worst nightmare is having a daughter who says she wants to sing. It was my mother's too! When I said to her, "I want to sing", she said, "Oh no!". She is of course very proud of me now, but she still has the same concerns and those are the same ones I'd have for a daughter of mine."*

*Prior to her meeting and falling in love with Bobby Brown and as a result their having daughter Bobbi, Whitney once said on the subject of falling in love, settling down and having children; *"One of the greatest moments in my life would undoubtedly be having a child, something that I really want. I've already had many great moments in my career, but nothing would beat that. I'd give up my career and spend two years looking after the baby. But I don't know if I've met the right man yet. We'll have to wait and see."*

WHITNEY ON HOW SHE GOT HER FIRST BREAK INTO THE MUSIC BUSINESS: *"It was when I did my first solo song, on a gospel record taped at church. Mum made me do it as I was always afraid to sing in public, but it went brilliantly. I was very nervous but it went well and now here I am today."*

At home with...

Whitney's constant hard work and the monetary rewards that it has brought has meant that she can practically choose wherever she wants to live at any given time. She has various homes but perhaps the most talked about is her 18 bedroom mansion near Mendham, New Jersey.

Whitney herself has said of the house in the past that,"*I wasn't actually able to live in the house itself until about three years after I first bought it because I was constantly on the road touring or doing promotional stuff. The house was decorated while I was away. I had the designers fly out to wherever I was and I'd choose the colours I wanted for various rooms. I put the house together with the help of my mother and when I came off tour was the first chance I had to properly move in. I gave a big party and everyone I knew came and that was actually the first day that I had ever walked into my own home. It was so exciting.*"

Exciting indeed, but not quite as exciting as the facts that surround the house itself.

Estimates of the actual cost of the house itself to be constructed and modified to Whitney's requirements vary greatly.

Everything from £5 to £15 million pound figures have been suggested. But whatever the actual cost of the house there is no denying its magnificence when looking at just what it consists of.

The construction itself is both unusual and unique There are practically no corners to the house as nearly all the rooms are circular. Also there are no solid walls as such as the house is predominantly constructed of glass creating a breathlessly light and airy feel. The glass windows are complemented by impressive silk curtains.

There are many stunning and innovative features that Whitney wanted to help make up her ideal home.

Inside there is a cinema, swimming pool and an imported Italian bath big enough to hold at least six people.

In the house's impressive entrance hall there is said to be a huge waterfall decorated with vines and flowers.

The huge living room is dominated by a circular couch and an ornate purple glass table.

A specially constructed conveyer belt linking the kitchen to the dinning room makes the laborious task of fetching food redundant as it does the job itself, whisking along food whenever it is requested.

Everything from the lights to the curtains are remote controlled giving the house an up to date and high-tech feel about it.

Outside, there's an Olympic sized swimming pool with Whitney's initials monogrammed in huge letters on the bottom.

When construction of the swimming pool was taking place in the grounds of the mansion she was asked whether she would like an oval pool, to which she wittily retorted, *"No, I want to swim in it not play in it."*

Also in the many acres of grounds that surround the property there is an observatory for watching the stars at night, a helicopter pad and floodlit tennis courts.

Back inside the house there is said to be among other features, a games arcade with all the latest features, an exercise and weights room, a roller skating rink and a state of the art recording studio.

Whitney's bedroom contains a huge circular bed which is usually adorned by scores of cuddly toys such as fluffy toy rabbits. Also contained within the room there are the luxuries of a high-tech gym, a sauna and a jacuzzi.

A walk-in closet is also incorporated which contains hundreds of Whitney's clothes and shoes.

Right next door is young Bobbi's nursery also sumptuously decorated and packed with lots to keep her amused, as well as every toy and game imaginable for her to play with.

Whitney and Robin, the truth....

Speculation has always been rife over the years as to what level of friendship Whitney's relationship with Robin Crawford had actually reached.

The truth of the matter seems to be that they have known each other from childhood, and, as in many other cases have merely remained very good friends over the years.

Of course, because Whitney is such a major name and can amply fill plenty of newspaper lineage, any little rumour or whisper has resulted in an extraordinary amount of coverage on this subject.

It has been said that certain quarters of the media, newspapers especially, will not write anything about anyone unless they can find something derogatory or malicious. This seems to have been the case on more than one occasion with regards to this part of Whitney's life.

Whitney has found herself in the position on countless occasions where in order to keep some form of sanity she has had to answer these allegations and questions in some way. This has taken the form of often answering the relentless questioning in a humorous way, but also on a number of occasions it does become apparent that she herself is very much fed up and bored rigid by the whole matter.

The rumours started very early on in her career when whenever she was seen out at a public function, or the like, she didn't appear to have any sort of male admirer with her.

Whitney herself though later explained in an interview just what a struggle her life was in the early days, with the constant touring and promotional demands that were being put upon her. And the result of this being that she had not in fact had anytime to pursue any sort of romantic life. She says, *"I wasn't really going out with anyone, (when the rumours started). I was on hold. I was touring. I was promoting. I was here. I was there. I didn't have time for anything else at all. A certain paranoia runs through you. It's not like when anyone met me they wanted to get to know me, because they thought they already did."*

About Robin Crawford, Whitney has been quoted as saying, *"Robin and I are very good friends, we've known each other since we were kids. People see us together and maybe it's because they don't know who I'm sleeping with, they say, 'Oh she's gay', not knowing what to say or believe."* *"All the rumours have placed a strain on our relationship at times. We have a working relationship, but we're also very, very good friends. And that's that."*

The problems had started initially way back in 1987 when during an interview for 'Time' magazine the subject was brought up. Whitney said, *"I know I'm not gay. When I first heard about this it hurt me because it was something being said about ME. I cried. It was not the fact or whether or not I was gay that was the problem, but because people were saying this and they don' know me. I realize the fact that this thing has been fuelled by the fact that I'm very private with my life."*

She continued on the same subject some years later, (and obviously by this stage from the tone of the interview very much fed up with the whole matter), this time in an interview with The Times newspaper, where she said, *"I don't care who's sleeping with who. But I've just become tired of dignifying the question with an answer, but that's my friend, (Robin Crawford), they're talking about and some-times it starts to get hard for her to have to deal with it to."*

Later on in the interview though, after again having to state the fact that, no she wasn't gay, but thanking you for asking anyway, she continued in a more reflective frame of mind and mused on the bewilderment she felt for the subject as a whole when she said, *"There's a sense in which all the things that have been said about me have kept people's curiosity up. And in the end this has made me more famous than I really am. In a very odd sense, maybe it's been beneficial to me. Like they say, 'Negative press is just as good as positive, 'cos it's all going the same way in the end - down the toilet'."*

Because of the pressures that the rumours had put on their friendship Robin Crawford herself has also felt the need on occasion to speak out on the subject, not just of the rumours between her and Whitney, but also about Whitney as a person and what's she like to work with.

On the first point, Robin has said, "*When I was younger I used to pray that I'd have something to contribute. I wanted to be needed, counted on. Well I guess I got what I prayed for, but I also got more attention than I ever bargained for. It's not easy trying to establish a career and be respected, knowing in the back of your mind that when you walk into a room, some people are thinking, 'That's the girl who...'. I've learnt to overcome that, but it's made me well known in a way I wouldn't wish to be. They are a bunch of liars though. I only have to answer to one person and it's nobody here.*"

On just how far Whitney has actually come since the early days when she and Robin would play in the streets together, Robin has been quoted as saying, "*The foundation that we had years ago, the friendship that we shared, is pretty much back there in the past. Now it's business. Those of us who work with her have to change to accommodate what happens. I'd say that, as a person, Whitney has pretty much stayed the same. I think it's the people around her, including myself, who've had to change. And a lot of times your feelings get hurt. I may look at her in a room and think, 'That's my best friend', but it's not about being that personal anymore. It's about going as far as she wants to go in her career.*"

Also asked about what changes and adjustments to her life she feels Whitney has had to make following her marriage to Bobby Brown, Robin is also very forthcoming when she says, "*None of us around her, not her mother, nor her father could be to her what a husband can be. In a marriage it seems to me that it is always the woman who has to do more - commit herself more, devote herself more, always be there. I think Whitney is going to be that kind of wife. She's very traditional and bible-written. And if that means changing anything about her, I think it will mean that she's going to take less shit. She's not high-handed or temperamental or arrogant, but although she walks softly, she carries an invisible stick. If you back her up against a wall, you'll be sorry. In the nicest way, she'll make you feel like this...*" (She then gestures by holding up a thumb and finger with the narrowest of margin separating them).

Part three

"The character I play, her name is Rachel Marron and she's a Rock star, turned actress. Her management decides that she needs a bodyguard, but she doesn't really want to know nor does she really care in the beginning. Her management knows that there's someone threatening Rachel's life. Rachel's not aware of it and they hire Frank Farmer (Kevin Costner) to protect Rachel. Frank re-arranges Rachel's whole life right before her very eyes, which she doesn't like very much and so there is a lot of conflict. There's a lot of conflict between the two of them in the beginning, but in the end they learn to respect and love each other and eventually they move on in their respective ways..."

A new challenge.

Whitney Houston's first foray into the world of films was to accept the lead female role in the film 'The Bodyguard'. Written some twenty years earlier by writer and director Lawrence Kasdan, 'The Bodyguard' was a romantic thriller which proved to be the ideal starting vehicle for Whitney's acting debut and the perfect spring-board towards future cinematic ventures.

The film's plot centres around the character of pop star Rachel Marron, (played by Whitney), who at the height of her popularity starts to receive a number of worrying and alarming death threats.

In a state of desperation Rachel's management hires on her behalf former FBI agent Frank Farmer (played by Kevin Costner), to act as her personal bodyguard.

Farmer is widely regarded as being one of the finest men within his chosen profession and in the past has guarded many top and influential political figures of the day, this included two US Presidents among his former powerful and important clients.

He has never before in the past *"done a celebrity"* and indeed has never in fact stayed in the employment of anyone long enough in the past for his *"feet to go to sleep"*.

Frank Farmer is a professional where his work is concerned and one who believes in having total control of a situation at any given time. He doesn't believe in leaving anything to chance and so every little detail is meticulously worked out and planned in advance. He takes control of everything where his clients are concerned, from their daily routines, to protecting them, advising them where necessary and generally seeking to reduce the odds of anything untoward happening.

But he is most undeniably viewed as the best his profession has to offer and so with all this in mind this is where the story starts to unravel in earnest.

The relationship between the two central characters is at first fraught and tempestuous to say the least, but events in Rachel's personal and professional life gradually help to turn the relationship between the two of them from an un-trusting and taut one, to an eventual falling in love of the two central characters.

Both Frank Farmer and Rachel Marron are top class professionals at the peak of their respective careers and neither is too keen on any interference from the other when they first meet.

This is all set to change, however, when following a series of written death threats and sinister letters, Rachel's and Frank's characters are brought together.

One of the film's more powerful and striking scenes revolves around the two's first meeting when after the initial dislike of each other is established, on Rachel's part, the need to have someone with Frank's talents around becomes apparent after a death threat on her life is thwarted by the ex -Secret Service man in particularly debonair style.

This actually proves to be by far one of the film's most engrossing and exciting sequences, along with a similar episode later on in which Farmer again comes to the rescue when a murder attempt upon Rachel is thwarted by the former FBI man.

Kevin Costner had first became aware of and interested in the script of *'The Bodyguard'* when filming *'Silverado'* in 1985, which writer Lawrence Kasdan directed.

Lawrence Kasdan had rapidly become one of the most sought after and respected writing and directing talents of the past decade, following his previous credits, which had included box-office blockbusters like, *'The Empire Strikes Back'*, *'Return Of The Jedi'*, *'Raiders Of The Lost Ark'*, *'Body Heat'* and *'The Big Chill'*.

The basic idea and first draft for the script of *'The Bodyguard'* had actually been started by Lawrence Kasdan twenty years prior to it actually being put into production, with Kevin Costner and Whitney Houston in the lead roles.

Back in the early 1970's, when Kasdan was still working as an ad copy assistant by day and working on and writing scripts by night, he conceived his first draft for *'The Bodyguard'*.

Originally the lead roles were written with the idea of Steve McQueen and perhaps Diana Ross filling them.

But despite intense negotiations at the time into the possibility of Steve McQueen and Diana Ross teaming up together, the project never got any further than the discussions stage and was eventually shelved for the time being.

Kasdan, though, thought he had something good within his screenplay and over the years he continued to both work on and refine the script.

In 1985, Lawrence Kasdan cast, the then relatively unknown Kevin Costner in his western, 'Silverado'.

The two enjoyed a productive and enjoyable working relationship during the filming of 'Silverado' and it was during this time that Kevin Costner first became aware of the script Kasdan had been working on for 'The Bodyguard'.

Costner was immensely impressed by what he had read and he began to deliberate the idea of helping Kasdan to turn the basic idea of the film into reality.

But due to other commitments and obligations, on both sides, it wasn't until some five years later in 1990 that either Costner or Kasdan were able to fully commit themselves to the project.

It was Kevin Costner's suggestion that they should produce the film together, through his company Tig Productions.

When talking with Kasdan about the script Costner mentioned how impressed he was by it, but also how similar he thought it was in places to the mid-seventies thriller, 'Bullitt', which starred Steve McQueen.

It was then that Kasdan confessed that he had in fact written the role with McQueen in mind. This was something that Kevin Costner had not been aware of, but was especially impressed by as McQueen had always been a hero of his and someone he had sought to aspire to in his earlier acting days.

When it came to the casting of the film's female lead, Costner was adamant that it should be Whitney Houston who played the role. Now all they had to do was convince Whitney of that.

The deal was offered to Whitney that as well as playing the role of Rachel Marron, she would also sing six new songs for inclusion on the film's soundtrack album.

Everyone involved in the films early pre-production stages was convinced that they had found a winning formula, tailor made for global success. But, initially at least, Whitney herself was tentative towards accepting the role.

When first offered the part of Rachel, Whitney was somewhat non-committal merely stating *"maybe"*, when asked if she would consider accepting the part.

Whitney herself later explained when interviewed why she herself felt an initial reluctance to accept the role. She says, *"I knew it was the right project, but Rachel's character had to be fleshed out a bit. In the first draft she was mean and bitchy all the time. I thought she should be a bit warmer."*

Eager to capture Whitney for the role the film's writers and producers agreed and hasty re-writes were ordered to soften up Rachel's character, but despite this Whitney would still not commit herself totally to the project.

Almost with a complete air of predictability, from the moment the world first caught sight of Whitney's looks and her obvious stage presence, the film world beckoned.

For years she was constantly offered scripts to read and parts in films before many even knew whether or not she could actually act.

Her name had become a big enough draw in itself and many producers and film studios were simply eager to snap her up and get her signature on the dotted line before each other.

Whitney herself though had very different ideas and was determined that she would only accept a film role if she herself felt totally happy with the part she was offered to play.

From early on in her career she was constantly linked with playing a part in the yet to be filmed screen adaptation of the successful Broadway stage musical *'Dreamgirls'*.

'Dreamgirls' which ran for a number of years on Broadway charted the rise of sixties sensation *'The Supremes'*.

It spawned a multi million selling soundtrack album and made stars of many of the cast, especially singer Jenifer Holiday. The planned cinematic version of the story has yet to be filmed but for a long time Whitney, as Diana Ross before her, was linked as being the ideal face, voice and presence to take centre stage and be the film's starring role.

Whitney herself was aware of the intense media speculation as to whether or not she would take a role in the film but was determined to accept a more challenging and demanding role than 'Dreamgirls' could offer.

She said, *"Everyone was talking about me doing 'Dreamgirls', it was like, yeah, we need someone who can sing and who looks good, lets get Whitney." But Whitney herself was convinced that "No, I didn't want to be a Dreamgirls."*

And so the rumours and speculation were set to continue along the lines that if she didn't want to accept the role in 'Dreamgirls', what part was Whitney going to accept? It almost became expected that she would take a role and accept a part in one production or another.

Accepting the role...

When Whitney was unsure of her authenticity as a potential actress and would not commit herself to the part, it created a dilemma for co-star Kevin Costner, who remained adamant that Whitney was perfect for the role, especially after having screen tested with her, and so was determined to secure her for the part at all costs whatever that involved.

In the end, that was actually to mean that the film was put on hold for a year to give Whitney time to be convinced herself that she should accept the role.

Even after two days of screen testing alongside Kevin Costner in Los Angeles for the part Whitney was still unsure.

Whitney later related her fears in an interview and also how she began to realise that she could actually take on and make a success of the role.

She said of the somewhat persistent advances by Costner to secure her for the role, *"I'd heard that Kevin wanted me for the part and that he was prepared to wait however long it took me to be available for it. That was tripping me out. I thought, "Why does this man want me so bad?"*

" Then after reading the script through thoroughly I began to see why. Rachel's a great singer, a good actress, she's up for an academy award - she's hot! Everyone loves Rachel. And I could relate to that because its been very much like that for me in my own career."

Whitney would later speak of why she was to become sure it was the right part for her to play when she said, about the character of Rachel Marron, *"She's a woman who respects herself. It's not often that you can find a role in which a woman can make decisions for herself. I know those women. My mother is one of them."*

Kevin Costner himself though still seemed to understand Whitney's dilemma saying that, *"I think she was scared because as popular as Whitney is, she takes an unwarranted amount of hassle from the press. She is a real big target for them and so if you combine that with the fact that she could turn out to be a bad actress, that's a huge risk for her to take."*

Costner remained determined as ever though to secure Whitney as his leading lady, and eventually was to achieve this through a series of personal phone calls to the reluctant would-be movie star.

Costner's assurances to Whitney that she would be a stunning success and that she couldn't possibly fail was one of the major influences in her finally accepting the role.

The other major influence on Whitney came from a close friend of hers who also convinced her that taking the role would be a smart move to make. Not just for her but potentially for others as well.

Whitney herself later explained the thinking behind this and the motives when interviewed saying that, *"It was something a friend of mine said to me that really helped me to decide on this and gave me the final impetus I needed to accept the role. She said, "Whitney, if you do this, do you realise what it will mean for other black actresses, for other black women, period? Immediately I was encouraged. She was right. It's a very, very strong role for a black woman."*

Because of Whitney's initial reluctance to commit herself to the project and the subsequent shelving of the film for a year, a couple of changes had to be made to the film's key personnel.

Most importantly perhaps was the realisation that the film's author Lawrence Kasdan would now be unable to direct because of previous signed commitments he had made prior to the film's delay. This meant a new director had to be found.

The job was eventually bestowed upon respected but relatively little known British documentary film maker Mick Jackson.

Although a largely respected and admired figure within the film world Jackson had not had a huge amount of experience however in the world of feature films.

His previous credits had included *'Chattahoochee'* and perhaps more importantly *'L.A. Story'* and it was his work on this film that convinced both Kevin Costner and Whitney Houston that he was the right man for the job.

One of the most admired and respected aspects of Jackson's work was the way he seemed to be able to get just the required performance from the actors involved and this proved to be one of the keys to the film's eventual success.

Mick Jackson was also one of the key people in helping and coaching Whitney Houston for her performance.

Producer Jim Wilson later summed up the importance to the film of director Mick Jackson,(after it transpired that Lawrence Kasdan himself, would not be able to direct it), when he said, *"We had discussions with Larry Kasdan about directing his own script, but he had already committed to another film. Then we found Mick Jackson, who we felt had a superb sense of style that matched our feel for 'The Bodyguard' and suddenly we were right on track."*

For Whitney, one of the biggest adjustments she was going to have to make according to Jackson was simply the transition necessary from being pop singer to becoming an actress.

Mick Jackson himself later reflected in an interview about his leading lady, the potential problems this could have entailed, saying, *"You're making a queen of her genre into a beginner again, and Whitney was aware of the loss of control that would mean". " Her life as a pop star means that everything is set to her requirements, which is totally different from what happens when shooting a film. When she first got to see the shooting schedule the first thing she said was, "I'm not a day person."*

Whitney herself was completely aware of the personal adjustments she would have to make to her own life during the two months of filming but readily admits that at times this proved to be something of a strain saying, *"It was the hurry up and wait syndrome that was difficult. I'd be there for six, seven maybe eight hours a day and then suddenly be told that "We're not getting to your scene today." And with me that was a bit of a problem, because I hate to be idle and there's always something else I could have been doing."*

Whitney Houston's eventual enormous success in the role of Rachel Marron and the large gross the film made at the box offices around the world was in part due to the obvious on-screen chemistry between its two leading attractions, Whitney and Kevin Costner.

Afterwards when interviewers asked Whitney about their on screen partnership she was always quick to praise Kevin Costner and state how much she enjoyed their working relationship. When asked how it was working with Costner she would reply, *"Very easy. He knew it was all brand new to me. He was very nice to me and helped me out a lot, everything was cool. I think he acts up a storm in this movie."*

Whitney and Kevin
The charisma and the chemistry

Whitney did indeed enjoy an excellent working relationship with Kevin Costner on the film, and this was to come across very much in later interviews when both were keen and quick to praise the other in ways that came across as far more than merely a publicity angle for the film, instead it did actually appear that they genuinely enjoyed each other's company and the process of working together.

In a series of revealing and intimate interviews for a variety of magazines both spoke of their experiences of working together on both the film and with each other.

KEVIN

In one such interview Kevin Costner was asked about the film itself and how he himself saw it, being as it was something of a slightly unexpected departure for him and his career at the time. He explained how he himself saw the film by saying, *"It's man and woman stuff. The more interesting movies are about men and women. It's hot and sexy - the ultimate work-out movie. The kind you would take your girlfriend to cos' it gets the batteries going a bit."*

Kevin Costner took his role as Frank Farmer in 'The Bodyguard' very seriously indeed, and in order to present the character in as real a terms as possible, under-went a whole indepth series of studied observations of real life bodyguards at work.

As well as talking to real life bodyguards, he consulted many security specialists about their work. Included in these was one of the most respected and well known Gavin DeBecker, who can list top politicians as well as movie stars and actors among his clients.

From his experiences of talking to these professionals, to his role in 'The Bodyguard', Costner would later say, *"I think this story rings true for many of us. There is a certain element that reminds us of our worst nightmare in terms of the public sometimes overstepping its bounds. It's something we all think about but rarely have a chance to express."*

On Frank Farmer, he says, *"Frank Farmer is heroic because he has a code and sticks to it. He is consistent, but not without fault. There is also a consistency to Rachel, because she is just as tough in her world as he is in his. But Frank shows her that she can relax and feel safe with him, and that changes their relationship."*

He was then asked about Whitney herself, did he specifically want her for the role? He said, *"I was knocked out by Whitney's talent on stage when I saw her perform. She has the necessary grace, charm and dignity to play Rachel. Like Barbra Streisand and Diana Ross she's such a classy, electrifying performer, the kind I think we all admire. It took me a whole year to get her to actually say yes to taking the role. I'd screen-tested her and I personally knew that she was perfect for the part and that she could do it, but she was (somewhat understandably) afraid she would turn out to be a bad actress and that was a huge risk. I promised her though that I'd be there with her and to support her and that she wouldn't be bad because I refuse to let anyone fail."*

Prior to his role in 'The Bodyguard' Kevin Costner had become over the previous eight years, one of the most respected, admired and in demand actors of his generation. 'The Bodyguard' was ultimately to enhance that image still further.

Kevin Costner made his official,(and probably the one he would prefer to remember), screen debut in 1981 in the Jim Wilson directed movie, 'Stacy's Knights'.

Before that, however, he had made a now infamous appearance in a low budget movie called 'Sizzle Beach'. Which, although he says is now a little embarrassing to look back on and remember, in retrospect it did in fact prove to be a valuable working experience at the time.

He has been quoted as saying, when asked about this subject whilst being interviewed in the past, *"'Sizzle Beach' was shot on weekends with my acting teacher as the director, but that experience helped me a lot in the long run. I suddenly knew what kind of actor I wanted to be."*

In the early days, like many other actors before him who also wanted to make a name for themselves, times were tough, and he had to struggle for any form of recognition and for the small amount of parts on offer

Whilst studying acting in his spare time, he was initially forced to take whatever work was on offer to help supplement his income. For Kevin this would usually take the form of working as a studio manager.

Eventually, he was to win a number of small or inconsequential parts in a number of films. Although his contributions would never always make it into the film's final versions, the experience he was to gain was nevertheless invaluable for the future.

His early credits included minor roles in such films as *'Frances'*, *'Night Shift'* and *'The Big Chill'*, which was coincidentally, his first opportunity of working under the guidance of Lawrence Kasdan.

His perseverance, and long term determination not to be a failure in any venture he attempted, was eventually to pay off for Kevin Costner when he landed his first major starring role in the film *'Fandango'*.

His starring role in *'Fandango'* made enough of an impression that he was also soon cast in major leading roles in a number of other films, all of which achieved a fair degree of praise and performed well enough at the box-office to convince others of his potential.

Among these earlier roles, apart from the aforementioned *'Fandango'*, he also appeared in a large capacity in films such as *'American Flyers'*, *'No Way Out'*, *'The Untouchables'*, *'Bill Durham'* and *'Revenge'*, all of which helped to enhance his growing reputation.

Perhaps his biggest break came when starring in *'Dances With Wolves'*. Co-produced with Jim Wilson, and released through their own Tig Productions company, the film was one of the biggest box-office success stories of the 1980's and was probably most responsible for Kevin Costner attaining the super-star status that he has today.

'*Dances With Wolves*' brought Kevin Costner worldwide acclaim and won him a string of awards as well. The film itself won seven Academy Awards, including perhaps the most prestigious of them all for Best Picture, taking the actor into a new realm of achievement with regards to American cinema.

'*The Bodyguard*', incidentally, was to be Tig Productions' second produced feature film.

Tig Productions, the company that Kevin Costner helped to set up, was named after Tiggy, his Grandmother, and has become over the years an outlet which allows him to be able to look at projects that maybe would not merit any form of cinematic release, judge them on their own merits, and then decide if he feels it is something he would like to pursue or not.

One such project that he decided he would like to become actively involved in through Tig Productions is an eight hour documentary series for American television called '500 Nations'. In it, he will narrate the history of the American Indians. He was partly inspired to do this following his experiences surrounding the making of '*Dances With Wolves*'.

Of this proposed series of documentaries, he says, "'*Dances With Wolves*' was one story, this will be the whole thing. I'm looking at different things to do through Tig Productions, not just big movies."

Asked if he would be interested in directing his own movie, Kevin responds, "*Yes, but I could only direct a movie that I'm totally in love with. Directing is time consuming and exhausting but I'm listening to my inner voices when it comes to picking movies, and so far I've been very lucky with the stuff I've done.*"

Lucky indeed he has been, or perhaps just very clever, as he has starred in some of the biggest and most successful films of the last few years. Included among these are the controversial bio-pic, '*JFK*', as well as the period adventure, '*Robin Hood: Prince Of Thieves*', and others such as '*Field Of Dreams*', all major success stories, in their own right, especially when it comes to box-office receipts at the cinemas around the world.

He has been called the biggest worldwide box office star of the decade, and when you bear in mind that the collective gross total of his films to date, is in excess of 1.3 billion dollars, you begin to see why.

Yet, away from all the Hollywood glitz and glamour and the paraphernalia that surrounds it, Kevin Costner often comes across, as, in his own words, *"Just an ordinary guy that got lucky."*

He appears to enjoy his stardom and the trappings that come along with it, but yet he often comes across in interviews as being just a little bit embarrassed about it all as a whole.

When speaking about adjustments that he has had to make to his life, and how it affects his wife Cindy, he says, *"The celebrity atmosphere I live with daily has changed me greatly. If I could change that, I would. I'm probably the worst guy all this could happen to, because fame doesn't help me pick the right script or do my job any better."*

" I don't like all the gossip that goes along with all this, and the entourage that follow you around. My life is so full of stuff that I really never bargained for."

Asked about the tag that he has so often been labelled with as being 'The Cool Guy', he says, *"That's the burden of movies. You always get the girl, you always say and do the right things. It's not like that in real life, at least not for me anyway. I've been completely embarrassed so many times in my life."*

Asked to elaborate on this, he continues, *"One time I was in Italy and a group of girls screamed at me from a bus. The traffic stopped and they all waved and were yelling at me. I tried to find something 'cool' to do, so I blew them a kiss. 'I'm so cool', I thought. Then I turned round and - bang!- hit real hard into a telephone pole. The girls all laughed and suddenly I was 13 years old again. Not such a cool guy."*

Asked what he himself was like as a 13 year old, he said, *"In many ways I was always a loner, I still am. Always on the outside, and I guess I went into movies because I wanted to give people enjoyment so that I could win them over."*

Continuing on this trivia based level, Kevin was also asked during the interview about his wife Cindy, and the interviewer wondered how he thought she felt with regards to the love scenes he has to perform in many of his films. He responded, *"She can hear these comments about what an interesting couple my co-stars and I make, but eventually she says bull to that. Her own response is that she and I are in fact a very interesting couple ourselves."*

Finally, when asked how he reacts to the criticism that his hairstyle received after its appearance in *'The Bodyguard'*, he says of sporting that particular cropped style, *"It's funny when people focused so much on my hair. It's been called The Haircut From Hell, but I'm not worried as my daughter said she likes it."*

And Finally.....

Five things you (probably) never knew about Kevin Costner

1. Kevin takes three lumps of sugar in his coffee.

2. During the tough early years, Kevin's wife Cindy supported the Costner household by earning a bit of extra money playing Snow White at Disneyworld.

3. Later on in their life together, after Kevin had become a big star, he paid thirty thousand pounds for a race horse as a present for wife Cindy.
The horse was named 'Proud To Be Together'.

4. Before becoming a major movie star and general heart throb to millions of women throughout the world, Kevin made an album as a member of a band called 'The Roving Boys'.

5. Kevin owned his first gun. which incidentally was a Winchester Rifle, when he was only five years old.

WHITNEY

Whitney herself somewhat mirrors Kevin's comments when she was asked if he helped her much with the role and the greater adjustments she was having to make from singing to acting, she says, *"He spent a lot of time with me helping me more than the director. He had promised to be there for me that's why I dared to do the movie."*

Whitney also goes on to explain that she was in fact able to help him with a couple of the film's scenes that were unfortunately eventually cut from the final version, she says, *"I helped him too - with the singing. The scene was cut from the movie, but at one point we had him serenading me with 'True Love Ways', a Buddy Holly song."* Perhaps the fact that this scene was cut from the final version of the movie was fortunate in the end as Whitney goes on to say that, *"He's a better actor than a singer!"*

She was then asked about Kevin himself as a personality and if she had actually met him before the idea of the film had ever arisen, she replied, *"I'd only met him once and was pretty bowled over actually because his charisma was incredible. It almost swamped me - the first time I met him I was stuttering like a kid. I was pretty amazed at the incredible aura he generated."*

One of the strangest adjustments Whitney had to deal with was the phenomenon of actually seeing herself up there 'on the big screen', she elaborates, *"It's intense when you're watching yourself that large for that long."*

Asked if she had undergone any intensive training or coaching before undertaking the role of Rachel, Whitney explains, *"No, I was willing to, but Kevin wanted me to be as natural as possible. It took me a while to be convinced but one day Kevin got tired of waiting for me to decide on the role and he called me and said, 'I want you to do this movie, what's wrong with you?' I told him that I was scared people would laugh at me but he said he wouldn't even consider doing the movie himself without me, and so that was important in me making my final decision to do it."*

The interviewer then enquired as to whether Whitney herself was similar to the character she played in the film and whether or not she herself had to employ the services of a bodyguard in the same ways that Rachel had, she said, *"I know her life (Rachel's), and I like her, I have a bodyguard that travels with me when I'm on tour or in public. But I don't have a bodyguard at home - maybe I shouldn't have said that. I've never been threatened by anyone though."*

As for possible future projects in the film world Whitney was somewhat coy when asked but did say that she still thought of herself as being primarily a singer and a performer and it was in that mould that she would be happiest to continue. However she did say that she thought it would be nice to make the occasional movie and that it was ultimately her ambition to star in an all black musical.

Finally she was asked what she herself thought about her own performance in *'The Bodyguard'*, she somewhat admirably managed to sum it up in just eight words stating, *"I think I did a damn good job."*

"COSTNER AND HOUSTON
SPARK TOGETHER
WITH A SPECIAL CHEMISTRY"
(Daily Express)

"CRISP AND COMPELLING STUFF"
(The People)

"TERRIFIC SONGS,
DREADFUL FILM"
(News Of The World)

"THE SOUNDTRACK WILL
SELL MILLIONS."
(Daily Telegraph)

"WHITNEY'S ON SONG
WITH AN OFF-KEY PLOT"
(Mail On Sunday)

"SHE MAY NOT BE
A GREAT ACTRESS,
BUT SHE'S NOT
A BAD ONE EITHER."
(The Independent On Sunday)

'The Bodyguard'
The Reviews

Much anticipation surrounded the opening of 'The Bodyguard', especially concerning Whitney's performance, the hype the film generated surpassed even her own previous standards that were achieved when a new album was imminent.

Prior to the film's general release around Christmas of 1992, the reviewers had already had a field day in many respects gladly pulling the film to bits and then throwing the pieces back up in the air to see if anything stuck.

Reviews of the film were varied to say the least. *"WHITNEY'S ON SONG WITH AN OFF-KEY PLOT"*, screamed the headline in the Mail On Sunday. Whilst the Daily Express' critic Ian Lyness was proclaiming *"COSTNER AND HOUSTON SPARK TOGETHER WITH A SPECIAL CHEMISTRY"*.

The aforementioned Daily Express critic Ian Lyness gave the film a more generally favourable review than some others describing it as a, *"flashy, efficient and occasionally taut thriller"*.

He goes on to generally praise the film and in particular Kevin Costner for not only undertaking the role, but for, in his opinion giving it *"enormous star presence"* and generally being able to lift it above the ordinary. He also goes on to praise Whitney on her debut performance suggesting she adds *"an engagingly extra dimension to what could merely have been a hackneyed pop queen portrayal."*

Tom Hutchison in The Mail On Sunday also has praise for Whitney, un-surprisingly most notably for her singing numbers, although he does go on to point out that although her character lacks enough positive direction and portrayal, Whitney herself shows plenty of promise for the future within her portrayal of Rachel.

The Daily Telegraph's reviewer took a far more cynical and cautious approach to the whole affair though proclaiming the film, *"a flaccid, overweight affair, notable chiefly for the much touted acting debut of singer Whitney Houston."*

Along with many other reviewers he does take exception to what is seen as a limited scope for portrayal within Whitney's part, although does concede that her performance is *"actually quite good."*

The People's reviewer William Hall though was far more impressed by the film in general calling it *"crisp and compelling stuff"*, and proclaiming Whitney's debut film performance as a *"real treat for her fans."*

Whatever the reviews the film got, good or bad, the real critics and the only true gauge of whether or not a film is a hit or not is of course the public.

They soon made their feelings on whether or not the film was a success or not though by flocking to the cinemas in their millions worldwide and helping the film and its subsequent spin-off sound-track recording to literally smash records worldwide with seemingly alarming regularity.

The over riding criticism of the film itself was reviewers' endless insistence that it didn't actually have a plot and what thin threads there were of one were inconsequential anyway. This though didn't affect the public's judgement in flocking to see it and it is perhaps Whitney herself who sums up just why the film is so appealing to a mass market who were perhaps becoming somewhat tired and blasé towards the previous Hollywood output of high action even higher body count blockbusters. *"Who's heart can't this movie touch?"* asked Whitney. *"We've (the public) been missing that level of 'Oh my God, I can lose myself in this movie. That's the key element. It's a film that isn't in any way offensive to anybody."*

And indeed that was what was essentially at the core of the film's success.

It was merely a return to the sort of innocence and non-offending story in the cinema screens that had undoubtedly been lacking for a number of years prior to this particular film's release.

'The Bodyguard'
What the papers said...

As could so easily have been predicted and expected, the various newspapers and magazines who seized upon the film's opening as a great newsworthy story would say there were many varied and conflicting reports regarding and discussing the film's merits and achievements and in some cases general lack of either.

"MEGA STAR
WHITNEY
IS SET FOR
A LONG STAY
AT THE TOP."
(Star)

"HER VOCAL TECHNIQUE
IS PHENOMENAL."
(The Times)

"SOME CRITICS CLAIM
THAT WHITNEY LACKS
THE EMOTIONAL
COMMITMENT OF HER
MOTHER CISSY AND
COUSIN DIONNE WARWICK,
BUT NOT ON THIS SHOWING."
(Hot Press)

"'I WILL ALWAYS LOVE YOU'
IS ALMOST WORTH THE PRICE
OF THE CD ALONE."
Manchester Evening News).

"MEGA STAR WHITNEY IS HEADING
FOR THE HISTORY BOOKS."
(The Sport)

"Despite the fact that everyone would
love to see me with my drawers down,
it ain't happening".
(Whitney Houston)

The phenomenal anticipation that was to surround Whitney Houston's acting debut in the estimated 37 million dollar production of *'The Bodyguard'* surpassed that even created by her albums.

Whitney was 'hot' in an extreme sense of the word and it appeared the whole world was clambering not just to see her first screen appearance for themselves but also to snap up the film's accompanying sound track album, to which Whitney had contributed six new tracks.

The Record Breaker...

Prior to both the film itself and the album's release, Whitney was again to score a new landmark in what was already by anyone's standards, a remarkable career.

On the 14th November, 1992, a single was released. *'I Will Always Love You'* was written by Country star Dolly Parton during the 1970's and had featured on several of her albums. It had already been released by Dolly in single form some years previously, and had also been featured in Dolly's '70s hit movie, *'The Best Little Whorehouse in Texas'* but it had not been the immense success that it was set to become when Whitney wrapped her distinctive vocal chords around the song's melody.

The song's inclusion in the film was not Whitney's idea, in fact the inspiration behind it was Whitney's co-star in the film, Kevin Costner, who had heard Dolly Parton's original version of the song some years before and had decided that it would make the perfect centre piece for musical inclusion in the film.

When the idea of recording the song was first put to Whitney along with a number of other titles she was not too keen and so it took a bit of persuading, mainly from Kevin Costner, that it was the perfect song and the one they needed.

When speaking about her eventual recording of the song for inclusion in the film some time later Whitney would say that, *"The song was suggested along with a lot of other titles. But it was Kevin who had singled it out. Although several other people had covered it he kept saying, 'This is the song, this is the one we need, it will be perfect'. So I kept playing it and playing it and eventually realised that he was right. I wasn't sure of the song at first, but know I really love it and think it was the right choice."*

The song took very little time indeed in becoming an international smash and forcing many countries to have to re-write the pop history books with regards to its many and varied achievements. Here are a few;

'I Will Always Love You'

* By February of 1993, the song had set a new record in America for achieving the longest consecutive run at Number 1 on the Billboard singles chart. It's 14 week run at Number 1 surpassed the 13 weeks that had only recently been set by Boys II Men with the song *'End Of The Road'*, who in turn had taken the record from Elvis Presley whose double A-sided single *'Don't Be Cruel/Hound Dog'* had held the previous record of eleven weeks at Number 1 for some thirty years plus after hitting the top spot and staying there resolutely seeing off all comer's throughout August 1956.

* The single topped the charts in over twenty countries around the world including Britain, The United States, Germany, Australia and Canada.

* It soon became the top-selling non-charity single ever in America by selling well over four million copies by early 1993. This figure surpassed that achieved by the USA For Africa singing stars whose charity single *'We Are The World'* was the previous biggest seller and meant *'I Will Always Love You'* was fast approaching becoming the biggest selling single ever rapidly catching the current record holder, the Band Aid single, *'Do They Know It's Christmas (Feed The World)'*.

* *'I Will Always Love You'* became the first single by an artist in over 21 years to go straight to Number 1 in the American Billboard singles chart from outside the Top 10. (The last song to achieve this particular feat was the Paul and Linda McCartney song, *'Uncle Albert, Admiral Halsey'*, a one week chart topper in 1971.

* It soon became the biggest ever selling CD single in Britain.

*With the single reaching Number 1 in America, that meant she became the first woman ever to achieve ten Number 1's there.

* As a result of the single's success in Britain and its durable run at Number 1 on the singles chart, Whitney picked up yet another record-breaking feat as she became the holder of the longest consecutive run at Number 1 in the British singles chart by a female artist. Ten weeks at Number 1.

Whitney the record breaker

The Bodyguard'

The success also of the movie's sound-track album, to which Whitney had contributed a total of six new recordings resulted in further honours and record breaking achievements. Among some of the accomplishments born out of the success of the album, there were;

*Whilst the single *'I Will Always Love You'* was enjoying its record breaking run at Number 1 of both sides of the Atlantic, the accompanying sound-track album to the film was released.
This was also rapidly to achieve Number 1 status at the same time, thus making Whitney the first ever artist in chart history to top the charts simultaneously at Christmas with an album and a single taken from it.

* The album topped the American Billboard album charts for over three months and in doing so this enabled it to become the fastest selling sound-track album ever, surpassing the previous long term holder's of this accolade which included the hugely

popular albums to two of the 1970's biggest grossing films, *'Grease'* and *'Saturday Night Fever'*.

* By February 1993, mainly due to the enormous success of the *'I Will Always Love You'* single, the sales of the album had been propelled to an impressive 15 million sales worldwide and an equally mind boggling 7 million sales in America alone. This had also enabled the album to score an un-precedented amount of Number 1's around the world, over twenty in all, which was to include attaining a Number 1 album in, among other countries, Australia, Canada, Germany, France, Japan and the United Kingdom.

* Two of the tracks to be found on the sound-track album to *'The Bodyguard'*, both being Whitney Houston recordings were singled out as nominee's for Academy Award's. *'I Have Nothing'* and *'Run To You'* were both nominated in the Best Achievement In Music - Original Song category.

* *'The Bodyguard'* film was also to make headline news for the records that it itself was starting to both break and create. Among those were the announcement that the film had registered the biggest weekend opening in United Kingdom film history, for the time, plus the film went on to become one of the five biggest grossing movies of all time.

Record breaking achievements of *The Bodyguard'* , both during its cinematic release and on home video rental:

At the movies...

* Following its release to the British public on 26th December, 1986, an estimated 5 million British cinema goers have been to see the film.

* The film took an estimated £17 million at the UK box office, well out-grossing any other film on general release at the time.

* On a worldwide basis, *'The Bodyguard'* now features as being one of the Top 5 box office grosses of all time.

And - on video...

* *'The Bodyguard'* enjoyed a record breaking first week of being available for video rental. During that first week there were an estimated 695,000 rentals of the video, which equalled 20% of ALL rentals that week.

* After five weeks of release on rental that figure had risen to 2.5 million.

* That figure of 2.5 million had also meant that in the five week period since its release an estimated 6 million people had seen the film on video.

'The Bodyguard' album

Following a hugely successful world tour, Whitney was to immediately embark on rehearsals for 'The Bodyguard'.

When selecting the material she would record for inclusion on the album, Whitney set out to try and choose the sort of songs that she felt Rachel Marron herself could well have recorded.

Rachel was a strong authoritative woman, and Whitney attempted to emulate that through the choice of songs, particularly such as the cover of 'I'm Every Woman'.

Whitney was very much able to 'feel' the role of Rachel through her own work. Having just come off an extensive tour, she had been through many of the situations that Rachel would find herself in during the film.

Because of this she was greatly able to appreciate what may well have been going on in the mind of the character she was going to play.

One of the key issues that Whitney was most able to relate to was the occasional necessity to have the presence of bodyguards around her, particularly while touring.

During Whitney's recently completed tour, she herself had to regularly employ the services of bodyguards in order to keep under control the thousands who she would encounter every night.

Through this she could begin to appreciate the important role they played in her life and the fact that should the occasion arise, they would be willing to lay their own lives on the line, for her. Praising those who undertake this profession, not just for her, but in general as well, she says, *"I have helped myself look at Rachel's relationship with Frank in the movie by remembering my own body-guards and the devotion they show to their jobs. It is a deep concept to me that someone would sacrifice their life for mine, but these guys do it without thinking. They are true heroes."*

The album to the film *'The Bodyguard'* was falsely looked upon by many as being in fact the new Whitney Houston album.

This though was not quite the case, despite the fact that Whitney was to contribute over six new recordings to the project. Her contribution to the album came with the songs, *'I Will Always Love You'*, *'I Have Nothing'*, a cover of the Chaka Khan disco classic, *'I'm Every Woman'*, *'Run To You'*, *'Queen Of The Night'* and *'Jesus Loves Me'*, the latter three all being brand new and freshly recorded songs.

Elsewhere on the album many of Whitney's contemporaries were featured along with a couple of more long standing and established artists.

The other tracks on the album featured established artists such as Joe Cocker who sang *'Trust In Me'*, and Aaron Neville who along with Kenny G contributed the track, *'Even If My Heart Would Break'*.

Kenny G also featured in a solo capacity on *'Waiting For You'*, whilst newer, more up and coming talents were also apparent in the form of Lisa Stansfield who sang *'Someday (I'm coming Back')* and Curtis Stigers, whose cover of the classic *'(What's So Funny 'Bout) Peace Love and Understanding'* was in many reviewers' eyes one of the albums stand-out tracks.

As had become pretty much standard practice by this time, when it came to the reviews for the album, as it would seem to with anything associated with Whitney Houston, the reviews varied wildly.

Whilst on the one hand the Northern Echo declared that the sound-track was, *"much better than most"*, Vox Magazine's reviewer, Gary Leboff was of the opinion that, *"Houston contributes six tracks to a ramshackle collection that suffers from the classic sound-track malaise, ie, the unspoken truism that all concerned are saving their best material for solo projects."*

Elsewhere, however, City Limits magazine proclaimed that, *"Whitney gushes gloriously on a clutch of diamantee encrusted soul soap operettas."*

Joe Jackson of Hot Press magazine gave the opinion in his review of the album of being most impressed by the 'feel' Whitney was able to give to her tracks on the album, she was credited as being it's executive producer.

He says in his review, *"From the opening song, ('I Will Always Love You'), Whitney immediately taps into her gospel base and that's the musical mode she explores in most of the tracks. She, (Whitney), clearly believes in setting her voice against a Spartan background, an approach that reaps rich rewards, particularly in ballads such as 'Run To You'."*

Of the other reviews of the album, the review at the more respected end of the market came from Blues & Soul, whose piece on the whole whilst being not all good or all bad at least was honest and gave a reflective account of Whitney's contribution to the album.

The review sums up Whitney's recorded efforts thus, *"Whitney's record breaking single open the album's account and remains, to these ears a carefully crafted but always contrived slab of pop slush and proceeds in similar style via the equally mushy ballad, 'I Have Nothing'. However, the lady digs her heels in finally with her very gritty version of Ashford & Simpson's 'I'm Every Woman', she then returns quickly to the emotive via the sugar sweet 'Run To You'.*

L.A. & Babyface contribute with a very noisy and rocky 'Queen Of The Night' whilst Whitney completes her stint with a slab of commercial gospel."

Whilst Whitney's contributions to the album were all firmly placed on side 1, Blues & Soul seemed equally if not more impressed in fact by what side 2 had to offer from the diversity of artists to be found there.

Of particular note from the tracks to be found on the album's second side, special mention was given to The S.O.U.L. S.Y.S.T.E.M. who's contribution to the album came in the form of a cover of the Bill Wither's classic, *'Lovely Day'*, which was given an updated feel from the more generally known original version courtesy of a spot of remix treatment by C & C Music Factory.

Also given a certain nod of approval was saxophone player

Kenny G. present on two of the tracks, the solo *'Waiting For You'* and the collaboration with Aaron Neville, *'Even If My Heart Would Break'*.

On the more negative side the album did receive an amount of criticism and bad reviews along with the good ones.

Among these included the review from The Daily Telegraph which described the album and Whitney as, *"Whitney Houston covers Chaka Khan's roaring proud anthem, 'I'm Every Woman' and I can't help feeling she'd deliver a Pepsi commercial with exactly the same inflections and emotional depth."*

So, as usual where Whitney was concerned, not everyone was particularly thrilled with what she had to offer, but of course this did little to deter the millions who went to see the film and bought the album alike.

Following on from the record breaking success of the *'I Will Always Love You'* single, the next single scheduled for release from *'The Bodyguard'* soundtrack album was Whitney's interpretation of a song Chaka Khan had all but made her own up to this point, the Ashford & Simpson penned, *'I'm Every Woman'*.

The release of *'I'm Every Woman'* had been scheduled in advance, but what no one had expected at that point would be that the date would in fact coincide, in the end, with the situation that the previous single *'I Will Always Love You'* would still be at Number 1 in the charts.

This led to the possibility of yet another record breaking feat being achieved by Whitney Houston.

Pre-advanced orders for the *'I'm Every Woman'* single had, up to just before its point of release, reportedly reached around the 70,000 mark. Bearing in mind the fact that at the time, in order to get a Number 1 single, a record had to sell anything between 50,000-150,000 many people both thought and expected that Whitney in fact would again be making chart history by becoming the first woman in the history of the British pop charts to replace herself at Number 1. *WHITNEY SET TO TAKE TOP SPOT FROM WHITNEY'* became a typical headline.

In the end the single didn't in fact achieve this feat, but still made an impressive first week showing on the chart, entering during it's first week into the top 10.

Released during February of 1993, *'I'm Every Woman'* was to get a surprisingly good response from the reviewers this time around.

Blues & Soul magazine summed up the general feeling surrounding the release of the single, when saying, *"if you were going to do something as madcap as cover a classic moment, then you would probably do it this way... making it very contemporary indeed, but also keeping that original spirit alive and kicking."*

The review also goes on to assess the numerous remix treatments of the song, for use in clubs, etc. And while they don't come in for quite the same praise, the overall opinion is still a complimentary one. *"It works and in spite of the fact that numerous house mixes have set out to destroy all that good work, the fact remains that what they originally did is happening, and is happening real well,"* the review concludes.

'I'm Every Woman' enjoyed a good deal of chart success in Britain where it eventually reached Number 4 in the charts during a lengthy residency. The record proved enduringly popular at both radio stations and on television where the video was afforded an unusually large amount of exposure.

The video itself was a talking point for many and soon became a much requested item when the opportunity arose. It had been shot in December of the previous year and chosen as the location for the shoot was an impressive looking former synagogue in the heart of Manhattan, New York.

The centre piece for the video was a performance by an all girl backing group and a selection of dancers who had been specially choreographed for the video by the same man who had worked the dance scene's in *'The Bodyguard'*. As a special bonus, Whitney had also persuaded her good friend Chaka Khan, who sang backing vocals on the song to appear in the video as well.

Following on from *'I'm Every Woman'* another single release was soon on its way, this time the power ballad, *'I Have Nothing'*. An Academy Award nominee in the Best Original Song category, *'I Have Nothing'* became a Top 3 hit for Whitney in early summer of 1993.

A further two tracks were released as singles from the album. First came *'Run To You'* in July 1993 and finally *'Queen Of The Night'*, a Number 14 hit when released during Autumn of the same year.

Part four

When Whitney met Bobby...

"Throughout all the madness and the hype and the peaks and the
cooldowns, I've retained my basic values.
Getting married and having children. That's old stuff -
but it's important to me."

Whitney Houston.

The above words appeared to have held a prophetic meaning
for Whitney Houston, as soon after she had made that statement
she was to meet the man who would become not only her husband
but also the father of her child, Bobby Brown.

For many years prior to her first meeting and subsequent
relationship with Bobby Brown the world's media had enjoyed a
veritable field day when it came to the subject of discussing
Whitney's romantic liaisons. For a long time rumours would constantly circulate as to whom Whitney was, or was not, as the case
may be, dating.

Many names were often thrown into the arena, but ultimately
dismissed as being unlikely, improbable and in some cases impossible. At any one point or another the media throughout the
world seemed convinced that Whitney was either madly in love
with or even about to elope with a succession of men ranging from
Robert De Niro to American football star Randall Cunningham to
a more widely publicised affair, but again one that ultimately led
to nothing, besides friendship, with film star Eddie Murphy.

When Whitney met Bobby however, something different was about to happen, something that would ultimately change both of their lives.

Whitney later re-called in interviews that first meeting and what initial impressions it helped them to form of each other. She says, *"We first met at the Soul Train Awards party and I kept hitting this guy with my elbow. Robin (Crawford, Whitney's personal assistant), came up to me eventually and said, 'That's Bobby Brown you're hitting there', I apologised and he said, 'OK' and gave me this really evil kind of look. When we first met although it wasn't love at first sight, it was certainly lust!".*

This initial meeting between the pair in which neither particularly took to the other at first was soon to lead, however, to a two year courtship between the couple, eventually to culmulate in their wedding which took place during the summer of 1992.

During this two year courtship the couple attempted at all costs to keep their romance and blossoming feelings for each other as far away from the prying eyes of the public, and more importantly the media, as possible. Around this time it had begun to become public knowledge that Whitney was in fact no longer seeing one of her former admirers, Eddie Murphy. However, despite referring to a new man in her life during an interview with 'You' magazine during November, 1990, she was still not prepared, as yet, to reveal the identity of the new man in her life. All she would say on the subject at the time was that, yes, she was currently dating someone, but she wasn't prepared at this stage to tell who he was.

Rather coyly, all she would reveal was that although he was not quite as famous as previous beau, Eddie Murphy, he was someone who very much existed and, *"he knows who he is and he's very much a man."* As a token of their friendship, she said, she now wore a ring he had given her, an ornate affair which she wore on the third finger of her left hand.

When the news came through to the world's media that this new 'special' man was in fact singer Bobby Brown many eyebrows were initially raised in surprise at the news.

The name is Brown...
Bobby Brown

The news of Whitney's romantic involvement with Bobby Brown spread through the world's newspapers and magazines like fire. As Woman's Own magazine accurately reported, *"She was the cool, sophisticated diva, seen as aloof and reserved with strong, spiritual beliefs... He was the raunchy sex machine, six years her junior and already the father of three children, each from different previous relationships. What could they have in common?"*

This was the question also being asked by a million other papers and magazines all keen for a scoop on the newly proclaimed couple and eager to divulge any little items of gossip that they could lay their hands on.

Many were suggesting their own particular reasons for the couple coming together, the fact they might in fact be in love seemingly the last thing on their minds.

A lot of speculators proclaimed that their involvement with each other was merely a hugely orchestrated publicity stunt, designed to revive both their respective career's to mutual benefit in different areas.

On Bobby's side the general impression that the media were eager to create was that he was desperate for publicity to help, in their words, 'his flagging career'. Although it was indeed true that he had a new album ready for release, his first for some three years, the performances of his previous, *'Don't Be Cruel'* album which had sold some five million plus copies worldwide would suggest that he neither particularly needed or desired publicity of this nature.

On the Whitney side, the story that emerged more often than others, and there were a different number of them, was that her reason for announcing her engagement to Bobby was an attempt to squash any rumours that she might be gay once and for all.

Whitney, of course, had heard all this before, many times over in fact and had now become relatively immune to what she regarded as being blatant un-truth.

In fact, later in interviews, Whitney would explain how she and Bobby found themselves highly amused by this latest round of media speculation on their relationship. She would go on to admit that, *"If you judge us purely on our public images, you probably would think that we're exact opposites as people. But you've got to know Bobby's family really to know him. They're very close, like mine. He has a strong spiritual background too. So all the things that really matter, we have in common."*

Whitney goes on to dispel any myths that might arise that she is unhappy about the image that Bobby Brown has by saying, *"I love that he has a bad-boy quality to him - but there's so much more to him that people don't always see... it can be pretty intimidating for a man to be with someone like me who has a famous name. But that doesn't matter to Bobby because he's so secure within himself."*

Bobby Brown's upbringing was certainly different to Whitney's strict Baptist one. The self-confessed former street hustler was raised in and around the area of Roxbury, a tough ghetto area of Boston.

Bobby's career had begun at an early age when he was a member of the teenage Jackson Five clones, New Edition.

However, this was not in fact Bobby Baresford Brown's first attempts at stardom. He had in fact made a sort of unofficial stage debut at the tender age of three when his mother took her young lad to a James Brown concert at the Sugar Shack venue in Boston.

He later was to recall in subsequent interviews how this 'stage debut' had come about when saying, *"It was during the intermission in James Brown's performance, his band was playing music and my mom pushed me on stage and told me to dance. That was the first time I was on stage."*

Bobby Brown was born on 5th February, 1969 and raised for the most part of his early life in the tough ghetto area of Roxbury, Boston.

His mother was a school teacher and his father a construction worker at the time. Bobby's childhood was little different in the early years from the other children in the neighbourhood. Being a tough area and with high levels of unemployment and redundancy little was on offer to the children of the area. His early years and indeed days were spent fulfilling the role of a self proclaimed street hustler. But it was always singing and performing to an audience that most harboured the thoughts in the back of his mind.

It was in 1980 that this idea first came very much to the fore front of his thoughts when, with the aid of friends and acquaintances, Ralph Tresvant, Ricky Bell, Ronald De-Voe and Michael Bivins he became actively involved with helping to form the nucleus of what was to become the successful early 1980's all singing, all dancing, teen group, New Edition.

The group was originally put together by the five members in order to take part in a local talent contest in Roxbury. First prize in the contest was a recording session with producer Maurice Starr, and in order to win this prize for themselves the group had devised both a medley of Jackson Five songs to sing along with an accompanying dance routine.

Despite the fact that the group did not in fact win the competition, they were in the end awarded the prize of the recording session with Maurice Starr on the grounds that they were a far more suitable outfit to record the type of material that Starr intended, as opposed to the Rap group who had actually won the competition.

As the prize for winning or at least being awarded the prize for the talent show, the group were offered a deal with the independently run Streetwise label.

Maurice Starr's idea surrounding the five members of New Edition was to turn and mould them into a 1980's version of phenomenally successful early 70's group, The Jackson Five.

This he set out to achieve initially by supplying the kind of material to New Edition that The Jackson Five would themselves have been likely to record early on in their career.

The process would also involve the group devising very similar dance routines to The Jackson Five and carrying the aura about them that they were in some way indeed an up-dated version of the aforementioned.

This idea was carried even farther forward when the time arrived for the members of New Edition to set about recording debut material for imminent release onto the American public.

A very similar sounding song, both musically and lyrically, was written, 'Candy Girl'. Sounding in part remarkably similar to a former Jackson Five worldwide chart topper, 'ABC', a hit all around the world in the early 1970's. The 'Candy Girl' single was not, in America at least, the instant success that Maurice Starr was initially expecting and hoping for. The group themselves were though, by this time, beginning to make a name for themselves in America due to both their live performances and appearances on American TV shows. In America the single peaked at a relatively disappointing Number 46, but in Britain it was to prove to be a different story completely as the single rose to the top of the British charts, reaching Number 1, for a solitary week in May, 1983, knocking the dire 'True' by Spandau Ballet from the summit of the British singles chart.

At first, the group proved to be hugely popular and constantly in demand in Britain, at least during the run of the 'Candy Girl' single in the British charts. However, their initial popularity waned when they were unable to comprehensively sustain and build on this initial success with their subsequent releases.

During the run of the 'Candy Girl' single in the charts the group were constantly featured in the teenage magazines of the time and would appear on popular British Saturday morning television shows via satellite links, etc.

However, the success was not to continue over a period of any particular longevity. Indeed, their next single, the follow up to 'Candy Girl' failed to capture the British public's attention in any way similar to its predecessor and was consequently only able to reach Number 43 in the British charts during a relatively miserly and disappointing five week run in August, 1983.

Coupled with this disappointing performance the accompanying album also failed to make any significant impact on the British album charts around the same time and so it appeared that a major re-think was needed for the group before beginning any further assaults on the record buying public.

With the group also failing in many ways to be able to sustain and build upon any early success that they had achieved in the

States as well, internal wrangles and arguments began to consume their time far more than recording or other such promotional commitments ever did. This was to reach the point of no return in 1984, when the group decided that on the back of their new found prestige and confidence within themselves and their respective abilities that they would sever their ties with Maurice Starr and attempt to go it alone on their own terms.

This splitting of the two parties, (New Edition and Maurice Starr)), resulted not only in New Edition seeking out and managing to secure a new contract on a larger scale than they had previously being offered with the Streetwise label, (when they signed with MCA records), but also started a period of intense legal battles with former guru Maurice Starr, over the group's departure from his control.

The legal hassles that the group were having to endure proved in the end to severely damage and hamper any chances that they may have had of building up a successful long term career, with it would seem most of their energies being put into minor hassles and problems related to their former manager, than into any subsequent recordings that they would make.

Following the group's decision to sign a new deal with MCA Records, they did however continue on their chosen path of the time and to record and score an amount of success with their records, although none was quite able to match the initial success and the level of popularity they had received with the 'Candy Girl' single.

In Britain, the group were to make one more visit to the higher echelons of the singles chart when their 'Mr. Telephone Man' single reached the Top Twenty of the British singles chart, peaking in fact at Number 19, during a nine week run in February of 1985. That though proved to be their last, (up to this point at least, as rumours of a possible coming back together and subsequent reunion for the group also seem to be surfacing), visit to the British singles chart.

In America, the group was beginning to build up a much more impressive and stronger following than before, and were beginning to make more significant inroads into the charts there. This peaked when their 'Cool It Now' single reached Number 4, becoming their first American Top 10 single in January of 1985.

However, relationships within the group were still somewhat frayed due to the legal problems that they had been enduring over the years, and following the release of their '*All For Love*' album during 1985, this was to reach breaking point when the group all but split totally and went their separate ways, with Bobby Brown being one of the first to quit, when announcing after the current album's release that he would be leaving to pursue a solo career.

Bobby Brown solo...
Out on his own

Following on from Bobby Brown's departure from New Edition he was indeed suddenly out on his own, thrust firmly into the media spotlight, the centre of attention and no longer merely one fifth of the focus that he once was.

He had managed to secure a solo deal with MCA Records having impressed enough people within the particular organisation of his potential due to his prior involvement and the amount he put into the group during his time with New Edition. However, the early period he endured as being a solo artist was not to be one of the most fruitful times of his career.

Having been a member of New Edition he was instantly tagged with that label and the subsequent early material he would record for release through the record company would very much reflect the sort of direction and material that his previous group were beginning to produce towards the end of his time there with them.

Having made a name for himself as part of New Edition he then found that actually shaking off the association he had made with that group would be a difficult proposition.

The record company and producers who worked with him on his early material were also very much aware of this fact. However, they in their wisdom had assembled and brought together for the project the sort of people around their new found solo artist that very much reflected the sort of output that was recognisable from the New Edition days.

This was to result in Bobby's first recordings as a solo artist emerging as very much a New Edition type sound and experience.

Of his debut solo album, 1986's, *'King Of Stage'* Bobby has subsequently said, *"It was really a solo New Edition album."*

This was to make the early years of his solo career particularly difficult as he was unable to form any real identity of his own and therefore unable to make any sort of significant impact on his own merits. He continued, when interviewed about this subject some years later that, *"The voice was there, the voice that they remembered from 'Candy Girl'. It didn't work out for me. We had to re-group and find out what my identity was as a singer."*

This was all reflected somewhat when the album failed in any real significant way to make much of an impact on the charts. The singles mainly fared little better. The most successful of these being *'Girlfriend'*, which in January, 1987 was able to climb only as high as Number 57 on the Billboard singles chart in America.

This was to lead to a major re-think as to what direction Bobby's solo career was going to take. However, no one involved wanted to merely sit around pointlessly discussing this matter, pulling the subject to bits, and instead work would soon begin on Brown's next solo album, 1988's *'Don't Be Cruel'*. This album would eventually prove to be the major turning point in Bobby Brown's career and help to mould him into the performer known throughout the world today. For the production of the *'Don't Be Cruel'* album Bobby was placed in the capable hands of acclaimed producers and writers L.A. Reid and Babyface who along with Gene Griffin would help to shape the sound and future direction that Bobby Brown's career would take.

The results of this working partnership proved to be completely different from any work Brown had completed before. The songs were suddenly harder, tougher with a more street wise feel and attitude and this also reflected upon Brown's performance of them. Keeping a dance element within the music proved to be crucial to their eventual success, starting within the club scene of the time and eventually comfortably crossing over to the pop charts as well as hitting their desired target within the black music arena.

123

The first single to be lifted from the album for commercial release was that of the title track itself.

Written by L.A. Reid and Babyface, *'Don't Be Cruel'* proved to be more or less the instant success within the charts that had been hoped for.

The single entered the American singles chart with little effort and by October of 1988 had reached the Top 10, peaking eventually at a very respectable Number 8. Instantly, it had seemed, the idea of partnering Bobby Brown with the Reid/Babyface/Griffin production teams had paid off and was going to lead to even greater success than had initially been expected.

On first release in Britain, the single did not however quite match the level of success that it had achieved in the States, reaching Number 42 on the British singles charts when released in August, 1988.

That was all to change, however, when the album's next single, *'My Prerogative'* was released during early 1989 and unquestionably paved the way for Bobby to emerge as a major new talent on a world wide basis.

Co-written by Gene Griffin and Bobby Brown himself, *'My Prerogative'* proved to be the single that put Brown's name onto the lips, not just of already established fans, but the public alike.

'My Prerogative' with its lyrical content believed to be referring to Brown's earlier split from both New Edition and his managerial team of the time, hit the nail firmly on the head, on a world wide basis where the public was concerned, as they took the song both to the top of the American charts and helped it become a top ten single in most countries that it was released throughout the world.

In America the song was released during October of 1988 and took just twelve weeks on the chart before hitting Number 1 and staying there for a solitary week during January, 1989. Its instantly infectious 'swing-beat' style proved to be enough of a temptation for audiences to also go out and buy the accompanying *'Don't Be Cruel'* album as well, as that was soon to follow the single's lead and soar sky-wards towards the top of the American Billboard album's chart.

In Britain the initial interest caused by the *'Don't Be Cruel'* single escalated to far greater proportions when *'My Prerogative'* was released. The song was an instantaneous smash and consequently stormed into the British Top 10, eventually reachingNumber 6 and enjoying an unusually long period of time in the British singles chart, eventually only bowing out after an impressive 17 week run.

The enormous success of the single in the British charts prompted the record company to reassess the *'Don't Be Cruel'* single which initially had performed quite as well as had first been anticipated. This resulted in *'Don't Be Cruel'* being issued as the official follow-up to the *'My Prerogative'* single, a move that proved to be the right decision when upon its re-release *'Don't Be Cruel'* suddenly took on a new lease of life and re-entered the British charts. Suddenly Bobby Brown was beginning to become a 'hotter' proposition as a solo singer than even those early halcyon days as a member of New Edition had bought.

With much of the American public displaying a particular penchant for ballads, at this time, whilst Britain was engulfed within its new found desire of encompassing dance trends, different singles were then released within the respective territories in order to maintain and capitalize on this success and attempt to break into the respective markets in a bigger and more long-term manner.

In America, the third release from the album as a single was indeed the slow paced ballad *'Roni'*. The song performed well, following as it did in the success of the chart topping *'My Pre-rogative'*. It eventually peaked at Number 3 in the Billboard singles chart during March, 1989.

In Britain, the re-issued version of *'Don't Be Cruel'* was followed into the higher echelons of the chart by *'Every Little Step'*, which was to provide Bobby Brown with his second Top 10 British single.

In the meantime the *'Don't Be Cruel'* album had also been re-leased in Britain and was beginning what would become a lengthy chart residency following its release at the end of January, 1989. The album was eventually to spend just eleven weeks short of a year on the British albums chart, remaining in the Top 75 for the greater part of 1989, peaking in the process at an impressive Number 3.

Due in part to the imposing chart performance of the *'Don't Be Cruel'* album and as a response to the new found popularity that

Bobby was enjoying with the British public during the year, MCA records also re-released Bobby's debut effort, the 'King Of Stage' album.

The 'King Of Stage' album, when first released failed to make any real impact on the British album charts, but as a result of this new surge of demand for Bobby Brown's material, when it was granted this re-release the album suddenly performed better than many had expected. Released in August of 1989, the album was to reach the British Top 40 of the album chart and spent six weeks on the chart in total.

Whilst all this was happening Bobby Brown was starting to get something of a name for himself, if not only always for his music. As a consequence of his new found widespread success and popularity he was soon to be found out on the road actively promoting the 'Don't Be Cruel' album by way of playing live concerts.

The nature of these concerts was often too much for some to handle and at times, Bobby's distinctly risqué performances were to result amongst other things in him being arrested after a show in Columbia, Georgia, for lewdness.

That aside, he continued to make a name for himself and the record sales continued to grow and grow. Primarily due to the enormous success of the 'Don't Be Cruel' album, by 1990 he had notched up a career sales total of in excess of six million albums, a figure that still continues to rise steadily up to the present day.

The 'Don't Be Cruel' album proved to be a rich source of future single material, although the next single he released was in fact a newly recorded song that was primarily recorded for use in the sound-track album to the film 'Ghostbusters II'.

Being very much in demand following his new found success Bobby had been approached with the view to recording a song for the 'Ghostbusters II' album. He agreed to this on one minor condition. He wanted a small part in the film. Due to his popularity a deal was worked out and he subsequently appeared in a minor role in the movie, playing a butler to the Mayor of New York.

This proved to be an excellent deal for all concerned as the song he recorded, 'On Our Own' went on to become one of his most successful solo singles to date.

In Britain the song was to become his highest placing yet in the British singles chart, reaching Number 4 in July of 1989.

Whilst in America, the song was kept at number two for three weeks by two different records. Initially Bobby was kept from reaching the top of the American charts by Prince whose *'Batdance'* single just prevented him from obtaining his second American number one single. Then, whilst the Prince single had fallen from the top spot after a solitary week spent there, Bobby again remained at Number 2, whilst being over taken for the Number 1 position in the process, by the Richard Marx single *'Right Here Waiting'*.

After diversifying from the album to accommodate the *'On Our Own'* single, it was then back to the album for the next officially scheduled release. In America, as in Great Britain this took the form of another of the album's slower paced songs, *'Rock Wit'cha'*.

The single was another American Top 10 single for Bobby, reaching Number 7 in the charts, but in Britain it was not to do quite so well, only reaching Number 33 when released in single form during September, 1989.

'Roni' was to prove to be the last officially released single from the *'Don't Be Cruel'* album in Britain when towards the end of 1989 the single was released and would go on to reach Number 21 in the charts.

Bobby Brown's next official single release was to return him not just to the upper reaches of the British singles chart, but would also see him taken back to the top of the American Billboard singles chart, courtesy of his duet with the Hawaiian born singer Glenn Medeiros.

Glenn Medeiros and Bobby Brown's partnership on the single *'She Ain't Worth It'* proved to be a fruitful one as the single went to the top of the American charts and was to remain there for two weeks in July, 1990.

Glenn Medeiros, whilst perhaps not regarded on British shores as being one of the most 'hip' singers around, was however, a huge success in America at the time, drawing thousand upon thousand of screaming girls to his sell-out concerts there.

His British Number 1 single *'Nothing's Gonna Change My Love For You'* had already also been a big hit in the States, but the duet with Bobby Brown was a move that surprised many neutral observers as well as industry types alike.

The original idea for the two to work together had actually come from singer Rick James, best known for his late seventies disco classic, 'Super Freak'.

Bobby Brown, who knew Rick James previously, later explained how the pairing of the two artists came about when he said during an interview, "Rick said he wanted me to work with this kid because he could really sing." He continued, "I knew he had the potential to become a great artist. I loved the song he did before, ('Nothings Gonna Change My Love For You'), and I used to sing it during my concerts. When I found out he did that song I really wanted to work with him."

Bobby Brown later continued on the subject of Glenn Medeiros in the interview, saying he thought he came across as being, "shy, kind of laid back. (Whereas), I'm always energetic, always up. It was like working with Michael Jackson, like working with a shy person, trying to bring out the rough side in him. And I think we did a pretty good job of doing that on the song".

Glenn Medeiros, for his part, later explained why he thought having Bobby Brown come in to add his distinctive style to the song was beneficial to the overall result, when saying, "I had finished recording the song, ('She Ain't Worth It'), and it was all but finished. We were going to throw in a rap of some kind into it. Rick James had talked to Bobby about it and after he agreed to do it, he came straight into the studio and wrote something there and then which went on the finished result and was perfect, just what we wanted."

Bobby Brown's third solo album was released after the news of his romantic involvement with Whitney became publicly known.

'Bobby' was the result of three years work on the singer's part and reflected a general consolidation in the sound and type of music he was best acknowledged for whilst it also attempted to progress and see him brought out more as a 'serious' artist.

This had a double-edged effect for Bobby Brown as many fans were of the persuasion of merely wanting more of what he had delivered before and as a consequence seemed unable to cope with the progression that the artist was attempting to make.

This was reflected by the album's relatively disappointing sales of both the album itself and its spin-off singles. Despite this though, the first single, *'Humpin' Around'* did see Bobby propelled back into the higher reaches of the American Billboard singles chart and also put him back into the Top 20 of the British singles chart, the song climbing as high as Number 19 when released as a single in August of 1992.

The greatest love of all...

It was around this time in Bobby Brown's career that he first became romantically linked with Whitney Houston.

Information regarding the relationship between Whitney and Bobby was not forthcoming from either of them in the early stages of their relationship, but eventually news began to filter out that, yes, they were indeed romantically involved with each other, and, yes, to the question of whether or not it was serious.

A large clue as to the identity of, at this stage, a mystery man in Whitney's life was confirmed when people started to notice that she was wearing a ring on the third finger of her left hand.

At this point in time everyone speculated, falsely as it turned out in the end, that this token of affection had been bestowed upon Whitney by long-term admirer and close friend Eddie Murphy. Eventually, however, the truth soon emerged that the ring had been given to Whitney by Bobby Brown and it was in fact he who seemed to be the man on whom Whitney was focusing her mind and attention.

Once the true story and the mystery behind the giver of the ring that Whitney wore so proudly had emerged, she herself seemed far more comfortable within herself and when later on in interviews, when the subject came up, she seemed happy, positively eager, in fact, to talk about not only the ring, but also the man who had given it to her.

When asked if the ring was in fact a sign of an engagement between the couple she was forthcoming when saying that, *"Bobby said it's for until he gets me a proper one. He wants me to have something else. To me, if he never gets me anything it would be fine. I know he loves me this is just one of the things that shows me that. I look at it and think, 'Ah, he loves me."*

The love that Whitney and Bobby had for each other was something that the two had been building and consolidating on for quite a while prior to either of them making the news public.

The news of Whitney and Bobby's feelings for each other were greeted with much surprise from many people, primarily because of the supposed differences between the pair. However, many felt deeply sorry for the two of them when the story emerged of how Whitney had suffered a miscarriage whilst filming *'The Bodyguard'*, earlier in their relationship, during the later part of the year in 1991.

Whitney herself would later talk in interviews very optimistically about this time in her life when saying, *"It was so sad, because Bobby and I wanted that child so much. At the time you wonder why it happened, but now I think I understand."* She continued, *"I'd found out I was pregnant when we were on location in Lake Tahoe, (filming 'The Bodyguard'). It was cold and we were living out of trucks - not the ideal situation. They were complications that my doctor and I knew about, plus I was trying to keep the whole thing quiet as well. But now, I believe that losing the baby was all for a reason, and God alone knows what that reason was. I don't question it. I just believe that it was something that was meant to happen and it wasn't the huge drama that it was made out to be - though obviously it was a very painful time in my life."*

It was actually soon after this event in their lives that Whitney and Bobby announced their plans to marry.

How Bobby proposed to Whitney was something that everyone wanted the answer to and Whitney didn't disappoint by relating the story whenever asked.

In one such interview she was asked, and replied, *"He was coming to visit me in Florida, where I have a home and he told me there was something that he badly needed to tell me. That freaked me out as I started worrying that he was going to say that he didn't want to see me any more or something. And then, when I picked him up at the airport, he was acting real nervous. Finally, I said to him, 'What's your problem?' and he answered by taking a tiny diamond ring out of a box and saying, 'Here, will you marry me?' I looked at him and said straight away, 'Yes, I will'. Then, just as I was about to put the ring on my finger, he laughed and said, 'You've got to be crazy!' Then he pulled out this other ring, which was much bigger and he asked me again...he loves to play jokes like that. I'd been thinking, 'Okay, it's a nice little ring - I'll put it on. Who cares?"*

She later continued on the same subject when saying, *"I knew that we'd both made the right decision there and then. I told him, 'You know you're the man I love."*

Later on, in the same interview Whitney was then asked if she was at all bothered when Bobby first proposed to her about the well documented fact that he had in fact been the father to three children previously, each the result of a different relationship. On this subject she said, *"That's all in the past and this is our future. He was young at the time. But I respect him because instead of being a punk about it, he was a man. He's taken care of his kids and spends a lot of time with them - they all just love their daddy."* She continued on this subject, *"Bobby said to me, 'They weren't planned, they were mistakes - but one's I don't regret, because I love my kids'. And I can respect that."*

Whilst the doubters and speculators continued to doubt and speculate about Whitney and Bobby's relationship the two of them merely went about the business of continuing to build on what they already had.

Many magazines were devoting countless coverage and space to the subject of the two of them, usually going along the lines of 'well this should scotch rumours about her sexuality' and 'this will help hype his first album in four years', very few it would seem could see any logical motive to the liaison.

Eventually, however, the media was to back off slightly on the subject and admit to the fact that it perhaps wasn't Whitney who had the problem all along, but that it was more likely, in fact, the media themselves, who had constantly refused to believe or indeed put to print anything about Whitney unless it was in some way malicious or derogatory.

The rumours about Whitney's sexuality would still occasionally surface and she wearily would again have to defend herself, although she was now starting to do that in a way that suggested that she herself was very sure of her situation and that if anyone else didn't after all this time, then they could just go away and amuse themselves with something else.

Whitney did seem very sure of herself and of her situation

when saying, *"The love I have for Bobby overwhelms me. We wanted to be with each other for the rest of our lives, so we got married. We were meant to be together." "But when I first heard these gay rumours it hurt me. I cried. It wasn't the fact of whether or not I was gay, but because the people who are saying these things don't know me and don't know anything about me. They were painful. The media is a big fat game and people make a lot of money out of it. The press seem to have a lot of fun with people like me. You know, at one point in my life, one minute I was supposed to be in bed with Eddie Murphy, the next I was a lesbian. I try to pay not too much mind to the lies, but sometimes it can still hurt. In the end you just have to retire into your private life and carry on the way you know things in fact are."*

During further interviews Whitney still continued to happily discuss both her imminent marriage and her feelings for Bobby Brown and the lengths that both of them appeared to want to go to sustain what they already had. On this subject she was quoted as saying, *"I'm not addicted to anything but love. It's fulfilling because you have to be so careful with it." "I've got money and I've got cars and I've got houses. Now I've got love and the things I do for love. I fly in the middle of the night on a charter plane from one coast to another and then back again. I've never had a relationship this strong." "I'm in love for the first time. I had no idea how it socked you. I don't know how to measure who loves who more. We are not weighing it that's far too far down the line."*

Continuing on the subject of her love for Bobby, she goes on, *"He encourages me, he's honest, he says what he feels. He's my man and he's my boy. He gets on my nerves sometimes, but he's my friend. We are comfortable. We are learning. I grab all the space and time with him that I can. God knows it's limited, but I just try to grab every piece." "I love doing 'normalities'. He gave me two akidas, (Lucy and Ethel, her pet dogs), for my birthday and they comfort me when I'm alone and apart from him.." "We met and it was like love at first sight. We've been dating two years now. I don't care what anybody says anymore. Lust comes into the first attraction. You don't look at somebody and go, 'Aah, that's a nice guy', you go, 'Wooh, I want to jump his bones'. I thought to myself when this all started, 'I'll just take what happens', and it happened to turn into something beautiful. This is forever, this guy's mine for all time, that's the way it is."*

The pattern of tiny feet

Following on from Whitney and Bobby's wedding it soon became apparent that a 'new edition', (excuse the pun), to the Houston/Brown household could be imminent.

Whitney has never made any secret of the fact that she adores children and has always intended to have her own, Bobby, it would seem, shared the same view.

In an interview Whitney spoke of her desire to have children with bobby that started the day they married when she said, *"I told Bobby on our wedding night that I wanted to start a family." " He said he'd have me pregnant before the ink on our thank-you notes was dry." " So we stayed in our cabin on our honeymoon cruise and made love all day and night. We wanted to make sure that we gave it our best shot. So there I was, suffering from morning sickness on our return. I never thought I'd be happy being sick to my stomach. But you bet I am! It's just what I wanted."*

It was indeed obvious that having a baby was, for a very long time, certainly something that Whitney very much wanted and something that would add just that little bit something extra special to her already glittering career.

In previous interviews she had always spoken intently and deadly seriously when the subject of having children came up and was eloquent when describing the scenario.

In the past, prior to meeting Bobby and becoming pregnant she would often say, *"I have been in front of millions of people over the years, singing my heart out, performing songs and that has been incredible. I've enjoyed every minute of my work and had some incredible experiences".* *"But in my heart I am conscious that I would like to have a good family life."* She continues, *"But I want to have children. I've done so much in my career, but the greatest moment in my life will be to have my child. I'd even give up everything and spend the first two years just looking after it. It's very important to me."*

When the news about Whitney's pregnancy was broken to the world's media, they acted in typically excitable fashion.

Whole articles were written, based solely around the topic and it became the expected headline news for many days after the announcement.

Many an article found its way across the Atlantic to British shores surrounding the imminent arrival.

These ranged from the trivial, as for example, speculation as to what colour the new arrival's nursery would be. To the more serious, yet still fairly flippant suggestion that the baby would be gifted, with allegedly, the richest couple in American entertainment for its parents. Estimations as to the couple's combined wealth at this time ranged wildly at anything between $50-150 million dollars. Or, 'that's an awful lot of diapers' as one publication choose to put it.

As for the parents themselves, Whitney spoke on the subject during an interview in December, 1992 with The Voice magazine, where she said, *"Bobby wants a baby girl - I just want a healthy child."*

Speaking of the possible problems that could arise due to both Whitney and Bobby having time-consuming and demanding careers, she said, *"It is going to be tough keeping a family together - even now it's hard when Bobby and I want to see each other and we can't. We're going to have to fit everything around our careers when the baby comes. I'm not planning to stray too far from home over the next year. I can record here, (from home), and make short trips, but that's it."*

Asked if she would be taking the baby along during Bobby's forthcoming tour, she exclaimed in surprise, *"Are you kidding! No, but I'll take the baby and we'll go see daddy when we get the chance! There's no question about that. No question at all."*

A baby girl for
Whitney and Bobby

That important moment in Whitney's life did in fact arrive on the 4th March, 1993, when with Bobby at her bedside at a private New York clinic, Whitney gave birth to a 6 lb. 12 oz. baby girl.

Fears had been expressed at one stage during Whitney's pregnancy about complications that could occur during birth due to Whitney's own health at the time. But a delighted hospital spokesman was elated to announce to the eager waiting press outside that, *"Both mother and daughter are doing very well. There were no complications and that birth went very smoothly."*

They continued, *"Both parents of the new born girl are delighted, everything was absolutely fine."* And then somewhat guessing what the next question from the waiting hordes would be, pre-empted them by stating, *"No, they haven't decided on a name yet."*

The news of Whitney's giving birth to a baby girl delighted fans and neutral observers around the world. Whitney had got her wish of becoming a happy and healthy mother to a beautiful baby girl.

Whitney and Bobby were both naturally ecstatic about the new member of their family and Whitney herself summed up her feelings on the subject later on when saying, *"When they put my baby in my arms for the first time I thought, 'This has got to be it', there's no better feeling in the world than this. It was an incredible feeling. I'm a mother and that's the biggest concern for me in my life right now."*

The birth of Bobbi Kristina, the name they chose for their baby girl, started a whole new chapter in the already remarkable career of Whitney Houston. Another goal had been achieved. The one that Whitney had most wanted.

A duet for love

As had been the case many years before, both with her mother, Cissy Houston and her aunt Dionne Warwick, the next big question surrounding Whitney's recording output was to be, 'When is she going to record a song with Bobby?'

Neither Whitney nor Bobby chose to dwell or elaborate on this subject in interviews, but at the back of their respective minds it seemed that it was something they intended doing together, but as with previous duets, with other artists, it appeared they would only be taking that step together when they both felt the time was right.

Whitney had the expected slowing down period of her career following the birth of Bobbi Kristina and in the mean time Bobby was extremely busy with his career, out doing promotional work for his eponymously titled album and playing live concerts at the same time.

They did however finally come together as a musical force with a song recorded late in 1993, and released in January, 1994, the aptly named 'Something In Common'.

In truth, 'Something In Common' was perhaps not the strongest song the couple could have chosen to make their recording debut together and this was partially reflected by its failure to climb higher than Number 16 in the British singles chart when released in Britain.

The song's accompanying video proved to the sceptics though, as if it were still needed, the couple's love for each other.

Partly shot in and around the grounds of their home it showed Whitney and Bobby displaying an undeniable degree of affection for each other.

The lyrics for the song were particularly poignant, despite the obviousness of the *'Something In Common'* title.

The first line, sung by Bobby was *'I know I may have made mistakes before'* and the song continued in similar vein with each of the pair singing a particularly poignant line for themselves before coming together in the chorus for a joining together... and a celebration of their married life so far.

British Discography

Albums

'Whitney Houston'

-TRACK LISTING-

TITLE   : *'How Will I Know'*
Written By   : George Merrill/Shannon Rubican
Produced By : Narada Michael Walden

TITLE   : *'All At Once'*
Written By   : Michael Masser/Jeffrey Osborne
Produced By : Michael Masser

TITLE   : *'Take Good Care Of My Heart'*
Written By   : Peter McCann/Steve Dorff
Produced By : Jermaine Jackson
Additional   : (Duet with Jermaine Jackson)

TITLE   : *'The Greatest Love Of All'*
Written By   : Michael Masser/Linda Creed
Produced By : Michael Masser

TITLE   : *'Hold Me'*
Written By   : Michael Masser/Linda Creed
Produced By : Michael Masser
Additional   : (Duet with Teddy Pendergrass)

TITLE   : *'You Give Good Love'*
Written By   : La La
Produced By : Kashif

TITLE   : *'Thinking About You'*
Written By   : Kashif/La La
Produced By : Kashif

TITLE   : *'Someone For me'*
Written By   : Raymond Jones/Freddie Washington
Produced By : Jermaine Jackson

TITLE   : *'Saving All My Love For You'*
Written By   : Michael Masser/Gerry Goffin
Produced By : Michael Masser

TITLE   : *'Nobody Loves Me Like You Do'*
Written By   : James P Dunne/Pamela Phillips
Produced By : Jermaine Jackson
Additional   : (Duet with Jermaine Jackson)

Additional information:

FORMAT: CD,LP,MC

CATALOGUE NUMBER: Arista - 406 978

RELEASE DATE: 1985

FIRST CHART ENTRY: 14th December, 1985

HIGHEST CHART POSITION: 2

WEEKS ON CHART: 119

'Whitney'

-TRACK LISTING-

TITLE   : *'I Wanna Dance With Somebody (Who Loves Me)'*
Written By   : George Merrill /Shannon Rubicam
Produced By : Narada Michael Walden

TITLE   : *'Just The Lonely Talking Again'*
Written By   : Sam Dees
Produced By : Narada Michael Walden

TITLE   : *'Love Will Save The Day'*
Written By   : Toni C
Produced By : Jellybean

TITLE   : *'Didn't We Almost Have It All'*
Written By   : Michael Masser/Will Jennings
Produced By : Michael Masser

TITLE   : *'So Emotional'*
Written By   : Billy Steinberg/Tom Kelly
Produced By : Narada Michael Walden

TITLE   : *'Where Are You'*
Written By   : LeMel Humes /James Calabrese/Dyan Humes
Produced By : Kashif

TITLE   : *'Love Is A Contact Sport'*
Written By   : Preston Glass
Produced By : Narada Michael Walden

TITLE   : *'You're Still My man'*
Written By   : Michael Masser/Gerry Goffin
Produced By : Michael Masser

TITLE   : *'For The Love Of You'*
Written By   : R. Isley/O. Isley/R. Isley/M.Isley/C. Jasper
Produced By : Narada Michael Walden

TITLE   : *'Where Do Broken Hearts Go'*
Written By   : Frank Wildhorn/Chuck Jackson
Produced By : Narada Michael Walden

TITLE   : *'I Know Him So Well'*
Written By   : Tim Rice/Benny Anderson/Bjorn Ulvaeus
Produced By : Narada MIchael Walden
Additional   : (Duet with Cissy Houston)

Additional information:

EXECUTIVE PRODUCER: Clive Davis

VOCAL ARRANGEMENTS: Whitney Houston

FORMAT: CD, LP, MC

CATALOGUE NUMBER : Arista 408 141

RELEASE DATE: 1987

FIRST CHART ENTRY: 13th June, 1987

HIGHEST CHART POSITION: 1

WEEKS ON CHART: 101

'I'm Your Baby Tonight'

-TRACK LISTING-

TITLE	: *'I'm Your Baby Tonight'*
Written By	: L.A. Reid/Babyface
Produced By	: L.A. Reid/Babyface

TITLE	: *'My Name Is Not Susan'*
Written By	: Eric Foster White
Produced By	: L.A. Reid/Babyface

TITLE	: *'All The Man That I Need'*
Written By	: Dean Pitchford/Michael Gore
Produced By	: Narada Michael Walden

TITLE	: *'Lover For Life'*
Written By	: Sam Dees
Produced By	: Narada Michael Walden

TITLE	: *'Anymore'*
Written By	: L.A. Reid/Babyface
Produced By	: L.A. Reid/Babyface

TITLE	: *'Miracle'*
Written By	: L.A. Reid/Babyface
Produced By	: L.A. Reid/Babyface

TITLE	: *'I Belong To You'*
Written By	: Derek Bramble/Franne Golde
Produced By	: Narada Michael Walden

TITLE	: *'Who Do You Love'*
Written By	: Luther Vandross/Hubert Eaves III
Produced By	: Luther Vandross

TITLE   : *'We Didn't Know'*
Written By   : Stevie Wonder
Produced By : Stevie Wonder
Additional   : (Duet with Stevie Wonder)

TITLE   : *'After We Make Love'*
Written By   : Michael Masser/Gerry Goffin
Produced By : MIchael Masser

TITLE   : *'I'm Knockin'*
Written By   : Rhett Lawrence/Benjamin Winans/Rickey
                   Minor
Produced By : Whitney Houston/Rickey Minor
Additional   : (Whitney's first credit as producer)

Additional information:

FORMAT: CD, LP, MC

CATALOGUE NUMBER: Arista 411 039

RELEASE DATE: 1990

FIRST CHART ENTRY: 17th november, 1990

HIGHEST CHART POSITION: 4

WEEKS ON CHART: 29

'The Bodyguard'
(Original Sound Track)

-TRACK LISTING-

TITLE   : *'I Will Always Love You'*

ARTIST   : Whitney Houston
Written By   : Dolly Parton
Produced By   : David Foster

TITLE   : *'I Have Nothing'*

ARTIST   : Whitney Houston
Written By   : David Foster/Linda Thompson
Produced By   : David Foster

TITLE   : *'I'm Every Woman'*

ARTIST   : Whitney Houston
Written By   : Nickolas Ashford/Valerie Simpson
Produced By   : Narada Michael Walden

TITLE   : *'Run To You'*

ARTIST   : Whitney Houston
Written By   : Allan Rich/Jud Freidman
Produced By   : David Foster

TITLE   : *'Queen Of The Night'*

ARTIST   : Whitney Houston
Written By   : Whitney Houston/L.A. Reid/Babyface/Daryl
                     Simmons
Produced By   : L.A. Reid/Babyface
Additional   : Co-Produced by Whitney Houston/Daryl Simmons

TITLE	: *'Jesus Loves Me'*

ARTIST	: Whitney Houston
Written By	: BeBe Winans/Cedric Caldwell
Produced By	: Whitney Houston/BeBe Winans

TITLE	: *'Even If My Heart Would Break'*

ARTISTS	: Kenny G and Aaron Neville
Written By	: Franne Golde/Adrian Gurvitz
Produced By	: David Foster/Walter Afanasieff

TITLE	: *'Someday (I'm Coming Back)'*

ARTIST	: Lisa Stansfield
Written By	: Lisa Stansfield/Andy Morris/Ian Devaney
Produced By	: Ian Devaney/Andy Morris

TITLE	: *'It's Gonna Be A Lovely Day'*

ARTIST	: The S.O.U.L. S.Y.S.T.E.M.
Written By	: Bill Withers/Skip Scarborough/Robert Clivilles/David Cole/Tommy Never/ Michelle Visage
Produced By	: Robert Clivilles/David Cole

TITLE	: *('What's So Funny 'bout) Peace Love And Understanding'*

ARTIST	: Curtis Stigers
Written By	: Nick Lowe
Produced By	: Danny Kortchmar

TITLE	: *'Waiting For You'*

ARTIST	: Kenny G
Written By	: Kenny G
Produced By	: Kenny G

TITLE	: *'Trust In Me'*

ARTIST	: Joe Cocker featuring Sass Jordan
Written By	: Charlie Midnight/Marc Swersky/Francesca Beghe
Produced By	: Charlie Midnight

TITLE   : *'Theme From The Bodyguard'*

ARTIST   : Alan Silvestri
Composed By : Alan Silvestri
Produced By : Alan Silvestri

TITLE   : *'I'm Every Woman'**

ARTIST   : Whitney Houston
Version   : (Clivilles & Cole House Mix 1)

* (AVAILABLE ON CD VERSION ONLY)

TITLE   : *'Queen Of The Night'**

ARTIST   : Whitney Houston
Version   : (CJ's Master Mix)

* (AVAILABLE ON CD VERSION ONLY)

Additional information:

FORMAT : CD, LP, MC

CATLOGUE NUMBER : Arista - 74321 16929 2

RELEASE DATE :

FIRST CHART ENTRY :

HIGHEST CHART POSITION : 1

WEEKS ON CHART : (still on chart at time of print)

British Singles

TITLE : *'Saving All My Love For You'*

CATALOGUE NUMBER : Arista ARIST 640

RELEASE DATE : 16th November, 1985

HIGHEST CHART POSITION : 1

WEEKS ON CHART : 16

TAKEN FROM THE ALBUM : *'Whitney Houston'*

TITLE : *'How Will I Know'*

CATALOGUE NUMBER : Arista - ARIST 656

RELEASE DATE : 25th January, 1986

HIGHEST CHART POSITION : 5

WEEKS ON CHART : 12

TAKEN FROM THE ALBUM : *'Whitney Houston'*

TITLE   : *'The Greatest Love Of All'*

CATALOGUE NUMBER   : Arista - ARIST 658

RELEASE DATE   : 12th April, 1986

HIGHEST CHART POSITION : 8

WEEKS ON CHART   : 11

TAKEN FROM THE ALBUM : *'Whitney Houston'*

TITLE   : *'I Wanna Dance With Somebody (Who Loves Me)'*

CATALOGUE NUMBER   : Arista - RIS 1

RELEASE DATE   : 23rd May, 1987

HIGHEST CHART POSITION : 1

WEEKS ON CHART   : 16

TAKEN FROM THE ALBUM : *'Whitney'*

TITLE   : *'Didn't We Almost Have It All'*

CATALOGUE NUMBER   : Arista - RIS 31

RELEASE DATE   : 22nd August, 1987

HIGHEST CHART POSITION : 14

WEEKS ON CHART   : 8

TAKEN FROM THE ALBUM : *'Whitney'*

TITLE   : *'So Emotional'*

CATALOGUE NUMBER   : Arista - RIS 43

RELEASE DATE   : 14th November, 1987

HIGHEST CHART POSITION : 5

WEEKS ON CHART   : 11

TAKEN FROM THE ALBUM   : *'Whitney'*

TITLE   : *'Where Do Broken Hearts Go'*

CATALOGUE NUMBER   : Arista - 109793

RELEASE DATE   : 12th March, 1988

HIGHEST CHART POSITION : 14

WEEKS ON CHART   : 8

TAKEN FROM THE ALBUM   : *'Whitney'*

TITLE   : *'Love Will Save The Day'*

CATALOGUE NUMBER   : Arista - 111516

RELEASE DATE   : 28th May, 1988

HIGHEST CHART POSITION : 10

WEEKS ON CHART   : 7

TAKEN FROM THE ALBUM   : *'Whitney'*

TITLE   : *'One Moment In Time'*

CATALOGUE NUMBER   : Arista - 111613

RELEASE DATE   : 24th September, 1988

HIGHEST CHART POSITION : 1

WEEKS ON CHART   : 12

(Not featured on any commercially released Whitney Houston album)

TITLE   : *'I'm Your Baby Tonight'*

CATALOGUE NUMBER   : Arista - 113594

RELEASE DATE   : 20th october, 1990

HIGHEST CHART POSITION : 5

WEEKS ON CHART   : 9

TAKEN FROM THE ALBUM   : *'I'm Your Baby Tonight'*

TITLE   : *'All The Man That I Need'*

CATALOGUE NUMBER   : Arista - 114000

RELEASE DATE   : 22nd December, 1990

HIGHEST CHART POSITION : 13

WEEKS ON CHART   : 10

TAKEN FROM THE ALBUM   : *'I'm Your Baby Tonight'*

TITLE   : *'My Name Is Not Susan'*

CATALOGUE NUMBER   : Arista - 114510

RELEASE DATE   : 6th July, 1991

HIGHEST CHART POSITION : 29

WEEKS ON CHART   : 5

TAKEN FROM THE ALBUM : *'I'm Your Baby Tonight'*

TITLE   : *'I Belong To You'*

CATALOGUE NUMBER   : Arista - 114727

RELEASE DATE   : 28th September, 1991

HIGHEST CHART POSITION : 54

WEEKS ON CHART   : 2

TAKEN FROM THE ALBUM : *'I'm Your Baby Tonight'*

TITLE   : *'I Will Always Love You'*

CATALOGUE NUMBER   : Arista - 74321120657

RELEASE DATE   : 14th November, 1992

HIGHEST CHART POSITION : 1

WEEKS ON CHART   : n/a

TAKEN FROM THE ALBUM : *'The Bodyguard'* OST

TITLE   : *'I Am Every Woman'*

CATALOGUE NUMBER   : n/a

RELEASE DATE   : 20th February 1993

HIGHEST CHART POSITION : 4

WEEKS ON CHART   : 11

TAKEN FROM THE ALBUM : *'The Bodyguard'* OST

TITLE   : *'I Have Nothing'*

CATALOGUE NUMBER   : n/a

RELEASE DATE   : 24th April 1993

HIGHEST CHART POSITION : 3

WEEKS ON CHART   : 10

TAKEN FROM THE ALBUM : *'The Bodyguard'* OST

TITLE   : *'Run To You'*

CATALOGUE NUMBER   : n/a

RELEASE DATE   : 31st July 1993

HIGHEST CHART POSITION : 15

WEEKS ON CHART   : 6

TAKEN FROM THE ALBUM : *'The Bodyguard'* OST

TITLE : *'Queen Of The Night'*

CATALOGUE NUMBER : n/a

RELEASE DATE : 6th November 1993

HIGHEST CHART POSITION : 14

WEEKS ON CHART : 5

TAKEN FROM THE ALBUM : *'The Bodyguard'* OST

Other projects on which Whitney has participated and as a result charted

ARTISTS : Teddy Pendergrass and Whitney Houston

TITLE : *'Hold Me'*

CATALOGUE NUMBER : Asylum - EKR 32

RELEASE DATE : 25th January, 1986

HIGHEST CHART POSITION : 44

WEEKS ON CHART : 5

TITLE : *'It Isn't, It Wasn't, It Ain't Ever Gonna Be'*

ARTISTS : Aretha Franklin and Whitney Houston

CATALOGUE NUMBER : Arista - 112545

RELEASE DATE : 9th September, 1989

HIGHEST CHART POSITION : 29

WEEKS ON CHART : 5

ARTISTS : Bobby Brown and Whitney Houston

TITLE : *'Something In Common'*

CATALOGUE NUMBER : n/a

RELEASE DATE : 22nd January 1994

HIGHEST CHART POSITION : 16

WEEKS ON CHART : 5

Acknowledgements

*Thanks to the following for help
with material source, etc...*

Arista Records.
Warner Home Video.
The British Library.

*Plus the following trade publications,
newspapers, magazines and reference books:*

Hot Press - Echoes - Blues & Soul - D.J. - The Voice - Elle - Select
Q, - Time Out City Limits - Vox - Music Week - Now - Smash Hits
No.1 - M8 - Hi - Just 17 Woman's Own - TV Hits - NME - Melody
Maker - Sounds - Record Mirror - 'You' magazine - Music Industry
Research Organisation - The Daily Mail - Mail On Sunday
The Guardian - The Independent - The Independent On Sunday
The Daily Telegraph - The Time - The Sunday Times - Today
The Sun - The News Of The World - Sunday Magazine
Daily Express - The People - The Daily Mirror - The Sunday Mirror
The Star - Daily Record - The Sunday Post - The Glasgow Herald
London Evening Standard - Guinness Book of British Hit Albums
Guinness Book of British Hit Singles - The Billboard Book of
Number 1 Hits.

Photographs:

(i), (ii), (iii), (iv), (v), (vi), (ix), (x), (xi), courtesy Arista Records.
(vii), (viii), (xii), (xiii), (xiv), (xv), (xvi), courtesy Rex Features Ltd.